THE CORES OF STRATEGIC MANAGEMENT

The Cores of Strategic Management is a study of the analytic tools and processes involved in the formulation and implementation of strategic choices in realistic organizational settings. Students are required to integrate their functional knowledge and understanding of the global environment with the concepts and principles of strategic management to determine effective ways to resolve complex problems concerning the relationship between the total organization and its environment. Creative analytical skills and effective communication in light of current management thinking are emphasized.

Katsuhiko (Katsu) Shimizu is a Professor of Organization Theory and Strategic Management at the Graduate School of Business Administration, Keio University, Japan. Previously, he served the University of Texas at San Antonio for ten years. He received his PhD from Texas A&M University and his MBA from Tuck school at Dartmouth College. His research has been published in various top journals including *Academy of Management Journal*, *Strategic Management Journal*, *Organization Science*, *Journal of Management*, and *Journal of Management Studies*. He is serving the editorial review boards for the *Academy of Management Journal*, *Journal of Management Studies*, and *Journal of International Management*.

THE CORES OF STRATEGIC MANAGEMENT

Katsuhiko Shimizu

Routledge
Taylor & Francis Group

NEW YORK AND LONDON

First published 2012
by Routledge
711 Third Avenue, New York, NY 10017

Simultaneously published in the UK
by Routledge
2 Park Square, Milton Park, Abingdon, Oxon OX14 4RN

Routledge is an imprint of the Taylor & Francis Group, an informa business

Library of Congress Cataloging in Publication Data
Shimizu, Katsuhiko, 1963-
  The cores of strategic management/Katsuhiko Shimizu.
  p. cm.
  1. Strategic planning. 2. Management. I. Title.
  HD30.28.S4323 2011
  658.4'012–dc22
                                                                    2011009213

ISBN: 978-0-415-88699-4 (hbk)
ISBN: 978-0-415-88700-7 (pbk)
ISBN: 978-0-203-80635-7 (ebk)

Typeset in Baskerville
by Wearset Ltd, Boldon, Tyne and Wear

Printed and bound in the United States of America on acid-free paper by Walsworth Publishing Company, Marceline, MO.

SUSTAINABLE
FORESTRY
INITIATIVE

Certified Sourcing
www.sfiprogram.org
SFI-00555
The SFI label applies to the text stock.

Dedicated to
all the people in Japan
who have suffered greatly but never give in

All of the author's proceeds from this textbook will be donated
to the Japanese Red Cross Society.

PROLOGUE

A partner of Boston Consulting Group, a world-premier consulting firm, once told me, "There is no such thing as an inherently complex problem. Seemingly a complex problem is a result of a complex combination of simple problems." I totally agree with him and thus, my first class of strategic management typically starts as follows:

SHIMIZU: What is 3×2?
STUDENTS: 6!
SHIMIZU: How about 7×9?
STUDENTS: 63!
SHIMIZU: 785695×8893592?
STUDENTS: Muuuuu ... Need a calculator!

How many possible multiplication problems do we have? Trying to "memorize" every problem and every solution is a recipe for certain failure. If we understand 81 basic patterns, we can apply the basics to "any" math problem. It may take some time, but we know finding a solution is possible. The same idea is applicable to learning strategic management. There are so many different and complex problems in the world and new problems emerge every day. We cannot memorize all the problems and solutions. But if the basics are mastered and students learn how to apply these basics, it is almost assured that a solution (or at least an approach to find a solution) can be found for the problems, even the most complex ones.

An old Japanese proverb says, "Don't mix up a trunk with branches and leaves." My personal opinion is that we have many textbooks that have too many branches and leaves (or bells and whistles). This problem stems from the belief that more is always better. In the age of "the data deluge," we should start thinking of "less is better."

The basic idea of this book is that we need a text that focuses on the "trunk" or the "bare-bones core concepts" of strategic management. Although this text has some cases, the main purpose of these cases is not to add new information, but rather they aim to help students understand the core ideas more clearly.

CONTENTS

1

WHAT IS STRATEGY?

What is "strategy" or "strategic management?" There are many themes, different ideas, and even many different classes that use the term "strategy." People tend to believe it is better and more helpful to have the term "strategy" or "strategic" attached to their ideas. This is similar to the stock price phenomena in the late 1990s when people added ".com" at the end of the company's name and the stock price of the company jumped about 20%. However, it is probably fair to say that not many people understand the true meaning of "strategy" clearly.[1] For example, is it easy to tell how "strategic management" or "strategic information system" differs from "management" or "information system?"

There are many definitions of strategy. For example, Henry Mintzberg points out that there are ten ways to define strategy.[2] Nevertheless, there are some overlapping themes across all definitions. The intention of this chapter, thus, is not identifying and arguing what is the right definition of strategy. Instead, this chapter discusses what we need to understand in thinking about and developing a strategy for an organization.

To be short, strategy is about the future plan of an organization (or an individual). However, strategy is not just a plan. A plan of a family in terms of where and how to spend the next vacation is not a strategy. Similarly, thinking about how or what we will eat tomorrow or the next two weeks should not be called a strategy. However, a plan to spend next year trying to get into a prestigious MBA program or trying to get a job from a very popular investment bank can be called a strategy. What is the difference?

The word "strategy" is derived from the Greek *strategos* "the art of the general" in the context of war. Carl von Clausewitz and Mao Zedong are two famous people who discussed strategy. Essentially, strategy was used as a plan to win a war. By definition, winning a war is beating your competitor. To do so, you have to understand the strengths and weaknesses of your competitor as well as strengths and weaknesses of yourself.

When the concept of strategy is applied to an organization, we have to understand what war to fight and what it means to "win." This usually means setting a clear goal for an organization. To achieve the goal, we have to develop an understanding of our customers. Winning the business war is not achieved by beating your competitors directly. Instead, business wars involve the continuous battle of attracting more customers than your competitors do. To this end, in thinking about strategy, we have to understand

- the goal of the strategy (what war are we fighting? What do we want to achieve?)
- 3Cs (customers, competitors or competition, and the company or self).

Here for the sake of discussion, I propose one definition of strategy and further discuss the goal and the 3Cs that are imperative in thinking about strategy.

Strategy

Strategy is a future plan to achieve a certain goal. Strategy consists of (1) identifying target *customers*, (2) providing better or less expensive services/products than *competitors*, and (3) utilizing the strengths (uniqueness) of the *company*.

Sometimes, the term strategy is interchangeably used with a business model, which can be defined as a particular system to develop products/services in a way to serve particular customer segments better than competitors.[3] Because organizations are supposed to be going-concerns and thus "a war" is continuous in the business world, you have to continue to develop/refine a strategy. Thus, not only planning a unique business model, but also building and refining the business model can also be a future plan to win a war.

Goals

Goal, Vision, and Mission (and Some Others)

It is probably important to discuss how a goal is different from a vision or a mission. There are so many different definitions used in management that refer to a vision and/or a mission. According to, Jack Welch, a legendary former CEO of General Electric, a mission is about how to win in business, which sounds like strategy.[4] To not confuse people by proposing another definition of vision and/or mission, here in this book they are treated almost the same. The only difference may be the time span they are referring to. A strategic goal typically focuses on three to five years (sometimes fewer), while a mission and vision tend to focus on longer term orientations.

Importance of a Clear Goal

If asked about the goal of a company, responses such as, "maximizing shareholders' value," "increase sales," or even "satisfying customers" are often given. It is difficult to deny such goals, which also means such goals can apply to any company. However, under such a general goal, organizational members have little idea about what war they are in or what they want to achieve. There are three problems when organizational goals are too general or broad:

1   Unclear feedback. It is difficult to know whether a goal is actually achieved when the goal is broad. What does "maximize" shareholders' value mean? Moreover, to the extent that a goal is vague and broad, there are too many ways (or excuses) to say "we made it." Unless we identify a specific and concrete goal, it is difficult to obtain clear feedback to strive for achieving the goal.

2   Lack of stimulus. When a goal is broad, it reduces the motivational influence to drive organizational members to accomplish it. In addition to employees being confused about knowing what exactly they are supposed to do, a broad and vague goal also lacks the power to stimulate individuals' imagination. For example, how does maximizing shareholders' value (whatever it means) influence the everyday lives of employees? If a goal is imaginable in terms of "I want to be a part of a successful team," passionate employees work hard to achieve the goal.

3   Vague standard for modification. Strategy is a plan for the future. This also means that a strategy may need to be modified in correspondence with changes in external business environments including competitors' actions. If a goal is clear and concrete, it is less difficult to modify the strategy. When a destination is clearly shared, all employees have to do is find an alternative route to reach the destination. However, when the goal is very vague or broad, the goal cannot be a standard on which the strategy is modified.

In sum, a goal should be concrete and measurable so that it can easily be understood, it is clear if it is achieved or not, and it can be used as a standard to modify the strategy in accordance with changes in the environment. Moreover, the goal should be conceivable, yet also challenging enough to stimulate organizational members. One useful acronym in setting a goal is SMART: Specific, Measurable, Assignable, Realistic, and Time-related.[5]

From this perspective, a good example of a widely used effective goal is "to be number one in this market." It is concrete and measurable. Because you can actually see your competitors and their employees, you can conceive what you should do or what needs to be done relatively easily. Moreover, being number one sounds good and it stimulates a sense of pride. In the same token, "being a public company," is another concrete, measurable goal that is both financially and emotionally motivating.

Interestingly, once a clear and concrete goal such as being number one or being a public company is achieved, many companies have a hard time trying to identify the next goal. It is partly because the previous goal was very powerful and partly because too much energy was dedicated to achieve the goal and very limited energy was spent on thinking about the next steps. It is great to be accepted by a prestigious college, or becoming a publicly traded company but then what?

Growth

From time to time, a manager will say, "Quality is more important than quantity," "we want to be the best company, not necessarily the largest company." It is true that too much focus on growth sometimes makes a company "greedy" and lose touch with customers. But, it is also true that such statements are often made after a company failed in diversification or lost its number-one position in the industry to a foreign competitor.

Similar to "being number one," growth can provide a number of important and positive influences for an organization. It can be argued that most managers want to grow their company one way or another. Below, three major reasons are discussed.

First, if your company is public, growth is what shareholders expect.

> Stock price = today's profit (Earning per Share, EPR) × future growth potential (Price Earnings Ratio, PER)

If a manager cannot meet the growth expected by the stock market, the stock price goes down, often quite drastically. Even if a company grows by 15% per year, the same thing can happen if shareholders expected it to grow by 20%.

Second, size resulting from growth is one of the most powerful competitive advantages. Wal-Mart is a good example of how size leads to competitive advantage. Proliferation of brand is another positive effect of getting larger. Of course, larger organizations are less likely to go bankrupt than smaller ones (although it does not mean that large organizations cannot go bankrupt, as is the case with General Motors).

Finally, growth accompanies opportunities: more and bigger business opportunities. This aspect is particularly significant in the case of start-up companies. In a small company, the harder one works, the more the company grows. Employees work hard because it is intrinsically fun and rewarding. That is why many employees in small start-up companies work like crazy in a very untypical work setting such as their garage or dorm room.

At some point, growing companies hit a wall. It may be because of the maturity of the market, strategic mishaps, or the company becomes too big to grow. In many cases, employees lose passion and motivation, because they do not see direct feedback from the market. As a result, they turn their focus inside. Rather than seeing customers and competitors to identify opportunities, they peer inside the company to find problems. This is when energetic entrepreneurial companies become bureaucratic political organizations. Not making mistakes is regarded as having higher importance than taking risks and pursuing challenges. Once vivid and passionate organizational cultures are often replaced with rigid rules and cost-saving policies.

More than 15 years ago, McKinsey, another world famous consulting firm, emphasized the importance of growth in its company brochure. Simply put, it said, growth solves most organizational problems. Although this statement is possible, it was probably a little bit extreme and can be misleading. This is probably why such a statement is no longer visible. Yet, the importance of growth for an organization is unquestionable. While it is true that quantity may not substitute quality, the importance of growth and its positive effects on employees should not be underestimated in thinking about strategic goals.

3Cs (Customers, Competitors or Competition, and the Company or Self)

Customers

The importance of customers and their needs is obvious. Managers and business journals are often consumed with "customer satisfaction."

One very important aspect of strategy is *not* understanding the importance of customers, but understanding the importance of identifying *target* customers (or customer segments). Why is it important to identify target customers? If you say, "it is because every customer (segment) has different needs," you are not wrong, but not quite right either.

Although customer satisfaction is almost a mantra in the business world, satisfying customers is actually *not* very difficult. If, for example, Dell, in competing with Apple, starts selling an iPod-like gadget with high quality software for, say, $25, what would customers feel? I am sure that customers would feel very satisfied. What is wrong? Dell is likely to lose money, a lot of it!

Put it another way, running a business inevitably involves satisfying customers *and* making money simultaneously. If you try to satisfy any and every customer, it becomes difficult to make money. Thus, a company needs to find customers who are satisfied with what the company can provide and are willing to pay for it. More specifically, *a company has to identify customers (customer segments) who appreciate its uniqueness and will pay for it.* It is impossible to satisfy all customers above and beyond all competitors, and still make money.

The key premise of this discussion is the limitation of resources. No matter how large a company is resources are limited. If a company spends the resources to meet the needs of all types of customers, resources will be spread too thin. If a competitor focuses on a particular customer segment and uses all its resources to satisfy the particular customer segment, it will likely gain customers. This is what happened to department stores in comparison to specialty stores. In this way, *trade-off* or *deciding what is done as well as what is not done,* is a critical concept in thinking about strategy. Although it is great to capture all the customers, this will never happen. To the extent a company needs to compete with many rivals, some of which have more resources, identifying a certain customer segment and investing resources heavily on that segment is the only way for a company to differentiate itself and survive in the long run. *Trade-off leads to focus, which is the source of differentiation from competitors.*

Competition

As pointed out already, strategy is a plan for winning a war, thus competition should be at the heart of strategy. Interestingly, competition is the most neglected C among 3Cs in the classroom. It is probably because people tend to focus on improving services/products over previous versions of the same product, as opposed to improving over competitors' products. People often feel satisfied if they are better *than they were before.* Unfortunately, customers do not care how much improvement was made over past products or services. What customers care for is better service/products or less expensive service/products *than competitors.* Put yourself in the shoes of a gas station owner. You work extremely hard to slash costs and pass the cost savings to customers, say five cents per gallon. However, if your price is a few cents more expensive than that of the rival across the street, customers will fill up across the street at the rival's station. A company must always see itself as customers see it. What companies need to strive for is providing better/less expensive services/products than competitors, not better or less expensive products than itself at a previous point in time.

In relation, the standard to evaluate "better" should also be based on the perspective of customers. Technological excellence or objective functions may not always be important. It is well known that technologically superior beta was defeated by the VHS. A simple vinyl bag (from my perspective) made by Louis Vuitton is a few hundred dollars more expensive than rivals and still very popular.

It is important to note that better/less expensive services/ products are an important part of strategy, but not strategy itself. A strategy is not better or less expensive services or products per se, but a business model that makes it possible to provide or manufacture a better product or the same quality product at lower costs is a strategy. Think about Dell. Although Dell gave up its number one position in PC sales to HP recently,[6] the growth of Dell from its inception in 1984 is amazing. In 2000, it captured the number one PC sales spot in the US and became the world leader. How could Dell become the industry leader in such a short period of time and maintain the top position for a long time? Is it because Dell's PCs were cheaper? Did Dell use somehow less expensive parts to build less expensive PCs? Nope. A PC is essentially a commodity. Most of the parts are available to anyone. In fact, most of the key parts are exactly the same: microprocessor from Intel or AMD, operating system from Microsoft, memory from Toshiba etc. It is not its product but its business model (direct model) that made Dell distinct from rivals. By getting orders directly from customers (both corpora- tions and consumers) and assembling PCs after orders are received, Dell slashed costs associated with distribution, mini- mized the inventory costs (including costs of obsolescence), which can be huge when technological change is so rapid. Fur- ther, Dell developed a sophisticated logistics system that made it possible to obtain parts at the lowest price and reduce storage costs without risking shortages. These sets of activities consist of Dell's direct model. Because of the consistency of each of the activities dedicated to lower the cost of the product, rivals had difficulties in trying to imitate the system. For example, HP tried to sell PCs directly by skipping retailers, which played an import- ant part in selling HP's printers and inks. Obviously, major retailers opposed and the idea received limited investment.

The same principle can be shown in pharmaceutical com- panies. The key success factor in a pharmaceutical industry is coming up with an innovative, blockbuster medicine. But even if you come up with one, the patent will expire sooner or later.

Thus, the real importance within the pharmaceutical business is to develop an organizational system that enhances continuous generation of such innovative drugs. Obviously, this is not an easy task. Many large pharmaceutical companies find it difficult and rely on acquisitions of smaller, more innovative companies.

Company

IMPORTANCE OF STRENGTHS

The importance of being better than competitors was just discussed. It is sad if a company's initial success gives competitors a good hint for competitors' greater success. If a business model is easily imitated by competitors, a win is only short term (won a battle but not the war). Thus a company needs to develop a strategy and a business model with sustainable superiority (i.e., sustainable competitive advantage).

Yes, innovation is important and that is what most companies are looking for. If a company comes up with a breakthrough idea, it may be difficult for competitors to imitate quickly. Unfortunately, such innovation does not happen very often.

To be more practical, to win a war, a company has to use something unique. If a strategy is general and anyone can imitate it, most likely it will be imitated quickly. A flood of imitation is often noticeable once a particular product or service turns out to be successful. When a fast food chain started staying open late and gained some additional sales, almost all other chains adopted the late hours. Many iPhone-like products and Kindle-like products flooded the market after the initial success of these products. In other words, managers should not be surprised to see competitors trying to imitate successful products and services. Instead, what needs to be thought about is how to make it more difficult for competitors to imitate. To do so, a company has to focus on its strengths and uniqueness that are not available to competitors. In this sense, *the core of strategy lies in the strengths.*

In the case of Dell, the direct business model was unique and hard to imitate. This was partly because incumbent PC manufacturers used retailers, relationships with which prevented those manufacturers from entering into direct business with the end customers. From a conventional perspective, not having a distribution network is an apparent weakness for a PC manufacturer, but Dell made the weakness a strength when it introduced the new business model. Moreover, Dell continued to refine its logistics so that it became even harder for competitors to imitate the model. Both Apple and Amazon also maintain a lead in the market by establishing a distinct brand as well as making a large number of software products available (we will return to this point in the section on business strategy – first-mover advantages). By reversely engineering the iPhone or Kindle, competitors can make exactly the same or even better products (note that patents are an important preventer for imitation but engineers are very good at finding a way to escape from patents). It is not the product per se that enables a company to have advantages over competitors. It is the well-utilized (and often reinforced) strengths of the company that generate competitive advantages.

WHY WE ARE MORE SENSITIVE TO OUR WEAKNESSES THAN STRENGTHS?

Unfortunately, we are more sensitive to our weaknesses than our strengths. Think about your everyday life in school. You like numbers and you are very good at math, but not very good at foreign language. Or, you like marketing and dealing with people, but you are not very good at accounting. When you have final exams next week, what do you study? Most likely, you will not study subjects you are good at. Instead, you spend a lot of time conquering your weakness and increasing your average GPA (grade point average).

While fixing your weakness is important, there are fundamentally unique assumptions in the grades of school exams, which cannot be applied to the real world:

Assumption 1: No matter how good you are, the highest score you can attain is 100 points. However, in the real world, if you are "very good," most likely, you have less than a 20% market share. If you have a 30% share in the market, you will be called dominant. In many cases, "top" companies are often competing for a 10–20% range (one notable exception is Google, which commands more than a 60% share in US and worldwide). Moreover, a company may be able to utilize its strengths and enter new markets or even create new markets (as Starbucks did). Thus, a company's potential is virtually unlimited when it uses and extends its strengths.

Assumption 2: In school, as long as you are good, other students' grades are irrelevant. You get 100 points, regardless of the efforts of other students. In the real world, that is not the case. Whether you are good or not is a relative term. Competitors will make every effort to imitate others' success and outperform them. While a company works on fixing its weaknesses and spends fewer resources to further extend its strengths, the strengths may not be strengths any more.

Assumption 3: In school, average grade is important. You want to get an average GPA of 3.0 or hopefully better. In reality, though, customers are rarely concerned about "average." Think of a restaurant you would choose for dinner. If you do not have much time and you are hungry, McDonald's where quick service is guaranteed becomes a good choice. If you prefer gourmet food but have severe budget constraints, it is OK to sit in a very crowded place with poor service, as long as food is excellent and cheap. When you are on a date, you want to go to a very romantic place with nice service and food. Of course, you cannot complain about the price the restaurant charges you. Bottom line: if a business tries to increase its "average score," it may end up having little or no uniqueness. Not many people want to go to a restaurant that is all Bs, no Cs but no As. To gain customers, a company has to be distinct. As long as it provides a distinct value, there will always be customers who will like it.

Somehow, in school, we appreciate students who are "balanced." As a result, we tend to emphasize fixing weaknesses rather than developing strengths further. This idea is poor from a strategy perspective. Strategy is about strengths and trade-offs. Unless the allocation of resources is biased toward strengths, a company will lose its distinctiveness and will end up getting unnoticed as one of many similar companies.

HOW CAN WE IDENTIFY, DEVELOP, AND USE STRENGTHS FOR STRATEGY?

One may wonder if there is any strength on which strategy can be built, particularly when you are much smaller than competitors. How can we find our strengths? Compared with large rivals with abundant resources and skilled people, it may seem like we do not have any strength!

Let me repeat. We are trained and educated to be sensitive to our weaknesses. Thus, it is not surprising that we have a hard time articulating strengths. However, identifying strengths is one of the first steps to take in formulating a strategy. In doing so, the following three points are helpful:

Point 1: Strengths and weaknesses are relative terms. Even if you think you are not particularly good at one thing, if your competitors are even worse, that may be your strength. Toyota's hybrid technology that developed the best-selling Prius may still be an interim technology. Compared with electronic cars or even hydrogen cars, the Prius has both a gas engine and an electronic motor, which sounds awkward. Yet, because alternatives are not available, such awkward technology is good enough to be distinct.

Point 2: When you examine one by one, it might seem like you do not have any uniqueness. However, you may be able to develop a strong business model by combining those parts more consistently than your competitors. Southwest Airlines has been the most successful player in the airline industry for the last 30 years with its cost advantage. They did many things to lower the costs, including not assigning seats, no meals, not using agents, and using only 757 airplanes. If you look at each activity, it is not difficult to imitate. However, Southwest did *everything* to lower costs and continued to do so over the last 30 years, which makes it difficult to imitate. Also, think why it is not easy for the US basketball team with all star players to win in the Olympics.

Point 3: Strengths and weaknesses depend on what game (or war) is played. If you are really macho, you may be good at wrestling or weightlifting, but probably not at high jump. When the game changes your weaknesses may become your strengths and vice versa. Dell used its weaknesses in its lack of a distribution network by pushing the direct model. With the growth of the internet it is possible for a small firm to compete with large rivals with brick and mortar stores, similar to how Netflix was able to beat Blockbuster. Maybe you have no strengths from the perspective of the current rules, but you can change the rules and make your weaknesses strengths.

Again, strategy is built on strengths. Given the limited resources within a company, resources should be used to further develop strengths, not to fix weakness. By developing strengths, a company becomes distinct. By fixing weaknesses, a company becomes average. Who wants "average" that has no uniqueness? Strengths do not have to be big or obvious. The strength may be subtle and small, which is perfectly fine. All a company needs to do is to understand its strengths (and weaknesses) well, and formulate a strategy that uses the strengths so that competitors cannot easily imitate it.

Peter Drucker once said, "Thinking is very hard work. And the management fashions are a wonderful substitute for thinking."[7] It may be seductive to adopt a widely popular management technique, but it is unlikely to give you a uniqueness. No matter how hard it might be, strategy needs to be thought out with knowing one's strengths deeply.

CORE CASE: MCDONALD'S ARCH DELUXE

In 1996, McDonald's launched Arch Deluxe, a premium hamburger series targeting the baby boomer market. At the time, according to market research, 78% of people thought that McDonald's was for kids and only 18% said McDonald's was good for adults. McDonald's has been losing market share in the US. With the Arch Deluxe, McDonald's tried to regain the baby boomer customers who left McDonald's when their children became older.

In fact, McDonald's had been working on developing high quality hamburgers for a while. However, "fast food for adults" was a tough sell. Mac-lean, a low fat hamburger that was launched earlier, failed miserably after a five-year commitment. Not to make a similar mistake again, McDonald's spent two years developing the Arch Deluxe. A number of group interviews were conducted and various meats and ways of cooking were tried. To find the best mustard, 50 different mustards were examined.

Despite all of the careful preparation and a large amount of investment on commercials, the Arch Deluxe was never popular either among adults or among children. Within one year after the launch, the Arch Deluxe series was terminated.

Source: McDonald's; "McDonald's strikes out with grownups" *Fortune*, November 11, 1996.

What was the problem with McDonald's? To this basic question, there will be a number of answers from students:

Loss of market share?
Not being able to attract the baby boomer segment?
Not being able to respond quickly to the loss of the market share?

It is important to start thinking "problem" as objectively as possible. The magnitude of the problem is often exaggerated by mass media. Just because it is the front-page article of the *Wall Street Journal*, it does not necessarily mean that the "problem" is significantly influencing the bottom line. Moreover, the "problem" may not be controllable. Accordingly, it is important to find objective data such as stock price, sales, and market share to understand the problem as systematically as possible.

In this case, the starting point is the decline of the market share in the US. McDonald's believed that it was because they lost the baby boomer customers. As a result, two years and a large amount of resources were spent to solve this problem. And the Arch Deluxe failed.

What should have been done?

Arch Deluxe was not good enough?

More market research was needed?

When we observe a failure of new products, market research is carefully done in many cases. Probably, interviewees said they liked it, but they did not buy it at McDonald's.

Eating a hamburger is different from buying a hamburger at McDonald's. McDonald's is a special place. It is a place where kids enjoy eating and playing around. It is a place where we can get inexpensive food quickly.

Baby boomers are a big and growing segment (Customers). McDonald's is losing in the segment (Competition). Thus, we should launch high quality hamburgers baby boomers like. Probably, this is what top management at McDonald's thought.

By the way, what were the strengths of McDonalds (Company)? It has a number of stores in very good locations. The brand is very strong. However, the strengths were perceived among children and family, not adults. No matter how good the Arch Deluxe was, you would have lost your girlfriend or boyfriend when you took her or him to McDonald's for the first date.

The failure of the Arch Deluxe is a textbook case in terms of how important it is to consider all 3Cs simultaneously. Even if a lucrative market is growing and you invented a product that can compete with rivals, you cannot win the war unless you utilize your strengths. More specifically, you have to target customers that appreciate your strengths, which include fun, quickness, and inexpensiveness. McDonald's strengths are appreciated by kids and families, not adults. McDonald's just added new products targeting adults with the setting targeting kids and family. Although the story does not tell what happened to the kids and family segment, launching such an expensive menu would have confused the core customer segments (as well as employees). When you target a certain segment, you have to give up other segments. Trade-off is difficult, particularly when your non-target segment is growing and your competitors enjoy getting such customers. But it is the trade-off that makes a company distinct.

This story provides us with an important lesson:

If you want to make everyone happy, you won't be able to make anyone happy.

2

EXTERNAL ENVIRONMENT ANALYSIS

In the first chapter, what strategy is and what consists of strategy were discussed. Particularly, the importance of goals and the 3Cs (customers, competition or competitors, and company) was stressed. In this chapter, a company's external environments, which are related to the first 2Cs (customer, competitors) are examined. It is important for a company to select an attractive market in which the company sees a potential to prosper. We examine the last C (company) in the next chapter in terms of internal environment analysis. As explained by the case of McDonald's, a company cannot survive without competitive advantages, even in a very attractive market.

A company's external environment is very broad and composed of many macro factors. Such factors include change of demography (e.g., aging of population), economic conditions (e.g., good vs. bad economy, globalization, currency and trade issues), political environment (e.g., regulations), social environment (e.g., health consciousness, movement to environmental safety), and technological change (e.g., proliferation of cell phone). Although these are important, it is also time consuming to examine every factor in detail. It is probably practical to examine generally first, and then examine deeply when a particular factor is relevant or shows important changes.

A more immediate concern is the analysis and understanding of the industry a focal company belongs to. In many cases, changes in the macro environments influence a company through the changes in the industry structure. Moreover, industry structure may change without change in the macro environment when players such as competitors and suppliers make new moves. Accordingly, the remainder of the chapter is dedicated to industry analysis and explanation of the key concepts in relation to the analysis.

What is Industry?

Industry is a widely used concept. In fact, every time market share is discussed, it is the industry that determines the boundaries and size of the market (100%). According to the *Longman Dictionary of Contemporary English,* industry is defined as "businesses that produce a particular type of thing or provide a particular service." What does "particular" mean?

Let's think about McDonald's. Which industry does McDonald's belong to?

Hamburger?
Fast food?
Restaurant?

Is McDonald's competing with frozen pizza or sushi sold at a local grocery store? Maybe?

How about Starbucks? It is well known that McDonald's pushed its premium coffee by ridiculing Starbucks' pricy coffee. Then, yes?

Although "industry" is widely used, it is not easy to clearly identify which industry a particular company belongs to. Similarly, people use "market share," but what "market" really means is often determined conventionally and may not necessarily fit with reality. It is important to understand what assumptions and reasoning are used when someone is discussing market share of a company.

When industry is too narrowly defined, one may miss potential competitors and other trends that are very important to the focal company (e.g., if Starbucks is assumed to belong to a coffee shop industry, one may miss the moves for coffee by

McDonald's and Dunkin Donuts). Meanwhile, when industry is very widely defined (e.g., McDonald's is in the food industry), what needs to be analyzed is extremely broad. Given the limitation of resources, an industry analysis is likely to be very shallow and any useful insights might not be obtained.

There is no magic formula to define a company's industry. Accordingly, it is recommended that you first define industry based on conventional wisdom (McDonald's belongs to the fast food industry). Then, change the scope a little narrower (e.g., hamburger) and wider (e.g., restaurant) and see how tedious/ easy it is to analyze wider/narrower industry and how new insights may be obtained. In some cases, you may want to analyze multiple industries. In the case of McDonald's, your main focus will be the fast food industry, but the coffee shop industry is also worth examining, given the competition between McDonald's and Starbucks.[1] It may be more practical and effective to analyze multiple, narrowly defined industries than to analyze one widely defined industry.

Five Forces and Objectives of Industry Analysis

The "five forces" framework proposed by Harvard Professor Michael Porter is probably the most famous and useful framework for analyzing an industry.[2]

Before explaining the framework, a basic question needs to be asked: Why do we want to analyze an industry? Not limiting to industry analysis, it is always important to clarify the objective of the analysis.

In terms of industry analysis, there are typically two objectives:

1 To understand the attractiveness of the industry in terms of the potential to obtain high profits. This objective is particularly relevant when possibilities for entering the industry are explored.
2 To understand the structure of the industry. In relation to the first objective, a deeper understanding of the industry structure and relationships among players in the industry

will help decisions whether or not a company should enter this industry and/or what factors a company, both new and existing ones, should consider in formulating a strategy. This objective is important when the industry is changing or a company is exploring opportunities to change the industry.

It is important to emphasize that *any analysis is only a starting point, not a goal.* Industry analysis provides insights regarding the "current" attractiveness and structure, at best. An industry is analyzed based on past data and former events. Thus, industry analysis does not automatically highlight how the industry will change or what opportunities may be available in the future. Based on the analyses, a manager has to ask, "What implications can be obtained?" Five forces analysis of an industry helps managerial decision making, but it is not a substitute for it.

The underlying idea of five force analysis came from the famous supply–demand curve in economics, as shown in Figure 2.1. Essentially from a perspective of a focal company, the industry is attractive when supply is low and demand is high so that the company can enjoy a high price point resulting in high profit.

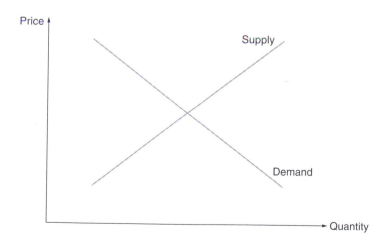

Figure 2.1 **Supply–demand curve.**

This basic idea is extended in three ways in the five force framework. First, supply and demand is a relative term. Think about McDonald's. It supplies hamburgers, but it demands beef, buns, and other forms of suppliers. In this sense, in thinking of a particular industry, you have to consider both suppliers to the industry and buyers to the industry in addition to the companies within the industry (rivals). Second, price (resulting in profit of a company) is determined not only by the overall supply–demand relationship, but also specific bargaining relationship between suppliers and buyers. When suppliers are powerful, they may charge a higher price, which squeezes the profit margin of the focal industry players. Third, an industry is not stand alone and static. Overall supply and demand can change when industry players increase/decrease or when buyers purchase something else that meets their demand. Customers may want to eat sushi or cook their own meal at home instead of eating hamburgers at a restaurant. Porter incorporated such potential by including new entrants and substitutes.

From the perspective of a participating company, an industry is attractive when:

1   rivalry within the industry is not intensive;
2   suppliers to the industry have little power;
3   buyers from the industry have little power;
4   entry to the industry is difficult (entry barrier is high);
5   substitutes (services or products) for the industry products are difficult to make.

In doing five force analyses, a logical first step will be identifying who the suppliers, buyers, and rivals are and if substitutes and entry barriers exist. However, the most important point is to understand the structure of the industry, i.e., relationship among the five forces. For example, power of the suppliers is not determined by the absolute size of the suppliers, but the relative size in comparison to that of buyers. In other words, arrows are more important than boxes in Figure 2.2. Figure 2.2

summarizes some key factors that determine the relationships.[3] The center oval is the focal industry (e.g., in the case of McDonald's, fast food industry or restaurant industry).

Power of Suppliers and Buyers

Suppliers become powerful when:

- costs for companies in the industry to switch suppliers are high;
- inputs provided by the suppliers are important and thus determine the quality and/or price of the products developed in the industry;
- when the concentration of the suppliers is high, resulting in less competition among suppliers;

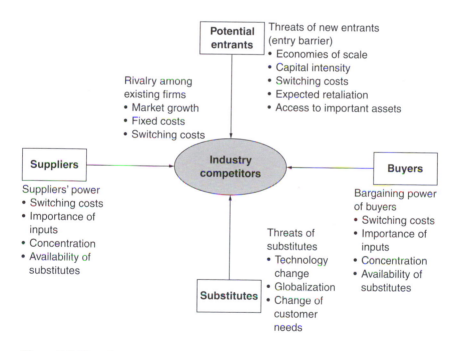

Figure 2.2 **Five forces and key determinants of the relationship** (source: adapted with the permission of Free Press, a Division of Simon & Schuster, Inc., from *Competitive Strategy: Techniques for analyzing industries and competitors* by Michael E. Porter. Copyright ©1980, 1998 by The Free Press. All rights reserved.)

- substitutes to the inputs provided by the suppliers are not available or are limited.

When one or more conditions exist, importance of suppliers to the focal industry is high, resulting in high bargaining power of suppliers. Suppliers typically charge a high price, which squeezes the profit margin of the industry.

The relationships with buyers are a mirror image of the relationships with suppliers. Thus, buyers are powerful when:

- costs for buyers to switch suppliers (firms in the industry) is low;
- inputs provided by the suppliers (firms in the industry) are not important;
- when the concentration of the industry is low, resulting in high competition among suppliers (firms in the industry);
- substitutes to the inputs provided by the industry are widely available.

Threats of New Entrants

From the perspective of incumbents, it is better not to have new entrants, who increase the intensity of the competition within the industry. The threat of new entrants can be determined by the difficulty associated with entering the industry called height of entry barriers. Entry barriers are high and thus a threat of new entrants is low when:

- scale is an important cost determinant of the industry and thus new entrants, which are often small, have difficulties entering and competing in the industry;
- entering the industry requires a large amount of capital;
- costs for buyers to switch suppliers (firms in the industry) are high, thus it is difficult for new entrants to obtain customers from incumbents;
- expected retaliation from the incumbents is high;

- access to important assets such as distribution channels and location is difficult, typically because the absolute number/amount of such assets is limited and the incumbents have already taken them or control them.

Threats of Substitutes

As discussed earlier, a definition of industry is always somewhat arbitrary. As a result, the distinction between competition and substitution is also arbitrary. Is pizza a competition for hamburgers or a substitute? It is not very fruitful to spend much energy on examining such a minor point. In many cases, we do not have to worry about substitutes, as long as we examine competitors in a relatively comprehensive way.

However, there are occasions when a whole industry is substituted and can become obsolete or the product or service is replaced. Think about the typewriter industry and the 35 mm photo film industry. The former was replaced by the PC industry and the latter was replaced by the digital camera industry. Similar phenomena seem to be happening in the CD industry (by online music industry) as well as book industry (by electronic book industry).

Such complete product or service substitution or replacement is often driven by technological change. Additionally, an industry in a certain area or country can be completely substituted by an industry in another area or country, most likely in developing countries such as China and India, although this is not substitution in a precise sense. To this end, it is important to follow the technology change and globalization in relation to the focal industry.

Industry Rivalry

As already discussed in relation to supply–demand curve, high competition among rival companies within an industry tends to result in lower prices which squeeze profit margins of all the firms in the industry. The intensity of industry rivalry is influenced by various factors:

- When switching costs are low, buyers can shop around every time they purchase. In this case, industry rivalry can be high as some firms try to maintain the current customers (i.e., building switching costs) and others try to attract those customers.

- Market growth declines or stops. When a market is mature, by definition, there will be a very limited number of new buyers. In relation to the switching costs, companies need to compete over a "fixed pie" or fixed market size and thus compete for existing (already someone's customers) with each other.

- The degree of fixed costs and storage costs also influence industry rivalry, typically through price competition. High fixed costs mean that a large amount of investment is already made in fixed assets such as manufacturing plants and airplanes. In an industry with high storage costs, keeping inventory is very costly. In both cases, a large portion of costs are predetermined, regardless of the number of actual customers or sales. Because variable costs (in this case, variable costs are marginal costs) are relatively small, a company wants to have as many customers as possible. Meanwhile, competitors think the same way. When one company slashes the price to attract rivals' customers, the rivals will respond and reduce prices even more to get the customers back. As a result, price competition to steal/protect customers intensifies until marginal revenue equals marginal costs.

It is important to note that competition is not always negative to an industry and/or to companies in the industry. Competition motivates companies to come up with higher quality/more efficient products/services. It is well known that companies in highly regulated industries tend to be inefficient (think of government offices?). Additionally, competition is good when the industry is relatively new. Amazon.com might have had to spend more time and energy if there had not been competitors. By having competitors, an industry increases its visibility among potential customers. As a result, the industry is perceived as legitimate more quickly. For example, think about taking a road trip across country using an interstate highway. Certain exits have many hotels and restaurants, while others have very few or none at all. Why? Travelers are more likely to pay attention to exits that have many hotels and restaurants than those that have very few. Of course, excessive competition will also hurt. As a result, the relationship between the number of competitors in a certain industry or area and the number of customers per company tends to show an inverted U-shape curve, as shown by Figure 2.3.

Switching Costs

Up to this point, switching costs have been discussed as influencing a number of the five forces (e.g., supplier power, buyer power, substitutes). Although switching costs are rarely examined extensively in a strategy text, it is and remains a very powerful and useful concept for understanding industry analysis. Understanding switching costs allows for an in-depth perspective on the actions of many companies.

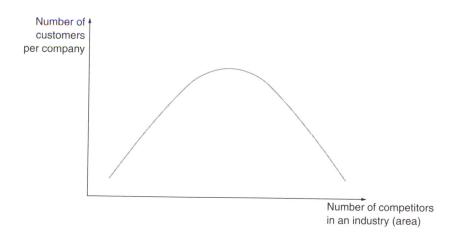

Figure 2.3 **The relationship between the number of competitors and the number of customers per company.**

Switching costs can be defined as "one-time costs customers experience when buying a similar product/service from a different supplier or a new product/service that has a similar function." Note that price of a particular product per se is not switching cost because a customer has to pay for it even if he or she is a first-time user. Switching costs are not limited to financial costs. When a consumer opens an account in a certain bank, they tend to stay with that bank for many transactions as opposed to switching to other banks even when another bank advertises very lucrative offers. Besides having to order boxes of personalized checks, it is a long, painful and inconvenient process to join a new or another bank. Forms need to be filled out, automatic deposits need to be rearranged, new bank cards need to be ordered and activated with new passwords. These inconvenience costs are a good example of non-financial switching costs. Similarly, many consumers keep using iPhones even when similar phones are available. Besides availability of software and tediousness to switch cell phone carriers, emotional attachment (I love it!) to a product plays an important role in preventing switch. Shampoo is another good example; many people use the same shampoo even when better or cheaper shampoo options exist. This is often because it is tedious to search for a better/cheaper one. Moreover, taking the risk of using a new shampoo can be a regretful one. Marketing people call such behavior inertial buying. The box below provides examples of different types of switching costs.

Examples of switching costs

- Monetary (e.g., replacement of a hardware/cancellation fees)
- Tediousness (e.g., learning/administrative work)
- Emotional attachment (e.g., personal relationship/brand image)
- Search costs/inertia (e.g., time)
- Risk (e.g., you may not like the new product)

As discussed in the five forces framework, switching costs can be high or low, depending on the industry. Although it is changing, the cell phone industry used to have very high switching costs. The costs included not only the cancellation fee but also the inconvenience of not being able to carry an old number to the new phone company. A consumer also has to tell all of his/her friends that their number changed (now you can carry the old number with a new provider). Contrastingly, switching costs associated with purchasing gasoline is quite low. Essentially, gas is gas, no matter where it is purchased. Many people buy gas either for convenience or for lower prices, although there may be some switching costs associated with the commuting routine.

When switching costs are high, it is good for companies to protect existing customers, but it is difficult to get new customers, particularly when an industry is matured and the only way to attract customers is to convince them to leave competing firms. As a result, competition to reduce switching costs arises. For example, cell phone providers offer free phones to lower switching costs not only because they can recoup the costs from the subscription fees but also to reduce the switching costs of users who already have a cell phone. Similar types of switching cost competition can be seen in cable TV and internet industries. Likewise, companies often give free samples of shampoos and foods to lower risks and uncertainties associated with switching.

Low switching costs can be good news because companies do not have to reduce switching costs to attract customers from competitors. But it can also be bad news. Switching costs are often low because services/products are very similar (i.e., commodity). As a result, the only difference can be the price and companies often end up in a price war, as experienced in the long-distance phone industry.

In such cases when switching costs are low, a company needs to try and increase the switching costs. One way to do so is to build a brand and create an emotional attachment to the products with customers. This technique is used by both Coke and Pepsi through extensive advertisements to promote "carbonated water with sugar." Another technique often used is the development of a "loyalty system" to reward repeat customers. Originally developed in the airline industry, such loyalty systems are very popular in many other industries including hotels, restaurants, retailers, credit cards, and casinos.

Finally, high switching costs suggest that it will be costly to attract customers away from competitors. In such an industry characterized by high switching costs, it is very important to attract first-time users. First time users tend to stay longer and provide a company with a much needed revenue stream for an extended time period. Through word of mouth, the customers may even bring other new customers.[4] This is why credit card companies (despite many criticisms) try to attract college or even high school students. When visiting a college town in August in the US, it is easy to see many banks offering very lucrative deals to attract freshmen as new customers who will stay in the town and use the bank at least for four years.

Recap

The idea of the five forces framework was first introduced more than three decades ago. Although it is still a useful tool to analyze an industry, it is important to understand the limitations as well. A critical limitation is its focus on competition: competition with rivals, competition with suppliers, competition with buyers, etc. However, after seeing the success of Japanese car manufacturers, the importance of cooperation is now well understood. Rather than bargaining with each other or viewing buyers and suppliers in a competitive light, suppliers and buyers can cooperate and achieve a "win–win" solution. One example is the relation between P&G and Wal-Mart. By sharing customer information, P&G and Wal-Mart have successfully increased sales as a team. Additionally, industry analysis has limited value when you start a completely new business and create a new industry.

The most important point is that *industry analysis is only a starting point, not an end goal.* If a company is considering entry to a particular industry, high entry barriers do not mean that it should give up. Instead, high entry barriers mean that a company will likely survive once it enters and establishes itself in the industry. The question is not just how high the entry barriers are but whether the entry barriers can be lowered. Similarly, high or low switching costs should not be taken for granted. After conducting the industry analysis, it is important to think about how to reduce or increase switching costs. Analysis of an industry is a raw material. Managers should use the raw material to develop a strategy to differentiate itself from others.

3

INTERNAL ENVIRONMENT ANALYSIS

In the previous chapter, external environments were discussed in relation to 2Cs (customers, competitors). In this chapter, we examine the last C, company.

An organization has various resources. In thinking about strategy, what resources a company has is less important than what resources are tied to its strengths. It is notable that the value of resources may not be clear until a strategy is formulated. Sometimes, the lack of a certain resource may become a strength, as Dell used its lack of relationships with distributors to build its core strength with its direct business model. In this sense, analyzing the internal environment and evaluating resources (in accordance with external environmental analysis) and formulating a strategy is not a linear, one-directional process. It is more of a back-and-forth, iterative process.

Sometimes, top management doesn't fully understand what they have or what they are good at. As the example of the Arch Deluxe at McDonald's from Chapter 1 shows, successful companies sometimes believe that they should be successful even in an area where they do not have enough resources to compete with others.

Value Chain

A popular framework to analyze an internal environment is the company value chain. This framework was also proposed by Michael Porter, back in 1985 in his second book, *Competitive Advantage*. The basic idea of value chain analysis is to dissect an organization into a series of value added activities or functions from obtaining raw material to sales and customer services. Overhead functions such as R&D, IT, and other administrative functions are added on the top as support activities.

The focus of value chain analysis is on understanding the importance of evaluating an organization function by function to identify which functions are strong and which functions are not. Because analyzing a company should be a systematic process, value chain analysis is a useful tool.

The value chain framework can also be applied to a higher level than an organization. For example, while a manufacturer of an engine can be evaluated using the value chain, an engine is a part of an automobile. When we think of an automobile as a unit, we can develop a value chain in which multiple companies are involved such as the engine manufacturer, the paint companies, the seat companies, etc. Given that alliances and partnerships are getting popular, such an approach allows us to evaluate a whole set of companies acting as a team to produce an end product, not just an individual team member (company) in terms of strengths and weaknesses.

Resources

A related but different approach to analyzing the internal environment is paying attention to the resources an organization has. There are two types of resources:

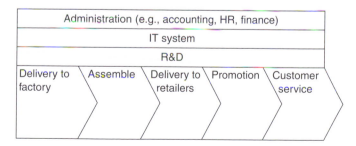

Figure 3.1 **An example of value chain** (source: adapted from Porter, E.M. 1985. *Competitive Advantage: Creating and sustaining superior performance.* New York: Free Press).

- tangible resources;
- intangible resources.

By definition, the former is something you can touch and see. Tangible resources include factories, distribution centers, and stores. Cash is also a tangible resource. In contrast, intangible resources are something you cannot touch. Although a factory is a tangible resource, knowing how to run a factory is an intangible resource. Employees are also tangible, but their knowledge, skills, abilities, personal connections, and motivation are all intangible resources. Other intangible resources include such things as brand, reputation, social capital, and organizational culture.

Importance of Intangible Resources

Although a company with a big headquarters and a large factory looks great, such tangible assets are generally not the source of competitive advantage. Instead, intangible resources are often more important in thinking about strategy mainly for two reasons.

First, tangible resources can often be obtained in the market. In other words, such resources are easily imitable. Meanwhile, since they are difficult to see and identify, intangible resources such as knowledge and skills are not easily imitated. Although one may argue that knowledge can be obtained by recruiting people with knowledge, an appropriate environment such as organizational culture and the relationships with other employees is often required to productively utilize such knowledge. Second, while tangible resources typically lose value or depreciate when they are used, intangible resources are not perishable. In fact, some intangible resources such as knowledge increase in value and amount as they are used. A company's brand can also become stronger or at least more identifiable when it is used. Existence of the many different kinds of Oreos in a grocery store is a good example of how powerful intangible resources can be.

Risks of Intangible Resources

It is important, however, to acknowledge the risks associated with intangible resources. It is difficult for competitors to imitate intangible resources because such resources cannot be seen or measured. With the same reason, managers and employees of a focal company also have trouble seeing or measuring the value of intangible resources. As a result, it is difficult to manage intangible resources appropriately for an extended period of time. For example, a cooperative and family-like organizational culture can be a strong competitive advantage because it can increase motivation and efficiency. However, such organizational culture can become insular or narrow-minded. Yahoo and PeopleSoft are two such examples. When Yahoo announced that it would hire a new outside CEO due to performance problems in 2001, the *Wall Street Journal* pointed out the "Insular corporate culture is source of many problems."[1] In the case of PeopleSoft, a fun, family-oriented culture attracted hard-working employees. However, as the company grew from 914 employees to 7032 employees in five years, "fun" was interpreted in various ways and employees' behavior spun out of control. One employee hit two people after drinking in the office. Additionally, the culture became exclusive and failed to incorporate new ideas from outside the organization.[2] "Experienced managers" hired from outside the company commanding exceptionally high salaries may leave the company in a few months sometimes because their skill was not as good as expected and sometimes because they did not get along with other employees well are also very common examples. Unless carefully monitored and managed, intangible resources that are supposed to be a source of competitive advantage can turn out to be a source of liability.

Economies of Scale

Although size of a company may not be called a resource, size can be a powerful competitive advantage over competitors through "economies of scale." Economies of scale are often defined as "a phenomena that larger size leads to lower costs."

Unfortunately, the mechanisms why larger size leads to lower costs are not well explained or understood in many cases.

Overall, there are three different mechanisms that connect size and cost. Here, size is indicating the number of units sold or the size of sales.

1   Fixed costs spread over volume. When a company manufactures or sells a large number of products/services, fixed costs of the company will be spread over the number of units sold for the product/service. For example, the costs of an airplane, fuel, pilots, and attendants, and the fee to use an airport are generally the same no matter how full an airplane is. When the airplane has a capacity of 200 passengers and 200 are flying, the fixed costs per passenger will be much lower than when the airplane has only 50 passengers. Advertisement of a new product is also a good example of fixed costs. If the same amount of advertisement was used and one product sells one million units and the other sells only 10,000, the advertisement cost per unit is quite different. In fact, such cost advantages of the former product will allow further investment on advertisement and other promotional expenses, which can further increase the sales gap of the two products. Other costs associated with overhead such as costs of headquarters, administration, IT, and buildings and factories are also

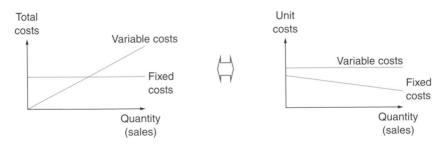

Figure 3.2 **Economies of scale: fixed costs spread.**

fixed costs. If the fixed costs are the same, larger companies enjoy lower costs per unit, and are able to pass the savings on to customers or use the savings for investments for future products.

2   Bargaining power to suppliers. As discussed in the previous chapter (five force analysis), a buyer ordering a large number of products from suppliers has a bargaining power over suppliers. Accordingly, a large company can potentially get a better deal than a small company. It is partly because suppliers can enjoy "fixed costs spread (e.g., factory, machinery)," when they receive a large quantity order. Moreover, suppliers also save some variable costs including sales costs (it is more efficient for a sales department to make one visit to one customer than five visits to five customers to get the same total quantity ordered). A large company (more specifically, a customer that places a large quantity order) is important for a supplier and thus can receive a better deal in terms of the price (and special delivery terms or rates) in many cases. Such a supplier–buyer relation is generally more frequent in the areas related to everyday operation (i.e., variable costs) than to one-time big purchases of some assets (fixed costs).

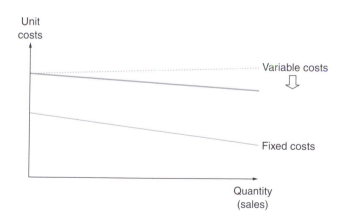

Figure 3.3 **Economies of scale: variable costs reduction.**

3   Experience effects. Generally, a company that manufactures or sells a large quantity of products has more experience in manufacturing and/or selling than a small company. Through experience gained, a company learns more efficient ways of manufacturing and/or selling, resulting in lower costs. The down-slope relation between costs and cumulative experience (typically curving due to diminishing return) shown in Figure 3.4 is often called an experience curve or learning curve.

Experience effects are also observed at an individual level. For example, suppose that you start a new job at McDonald's. Even if you read manuals (experience and learning are also a source of the manuals), your actual work remains relatively unsmooth and you may make mistakes in the beginning. After a few days, however, you can learn how to move efficiently and how to avoid mistakes. This is one reason high turnover in the restaurant industry is a big issue for management.

Many people discuss economies of scale without paying attention to the three different mechanisms underlying them. However, such casual usage may not be good for three reasons.

1   Specific costs reduced by scale are different. Fixed cost spread focuses on fixed costs, while bargaining power is typically associated with variable costs. Experience effects

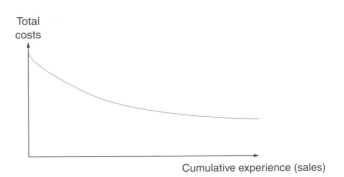

Figure 3.4 **Economies of scale: experience (or learning) curve.**

are costs associated with people, such as labor, sales, and R&D because it is people who learn and make things more efficient.

2 As a result, a strategy to compete with larger companies will be different depending on which source of economies of scale your competitors enjoy. Besides directly increasing sales by mergers and acquisitions (M&As), there are various ways to compete.

- If the fixed costs of manufacturing plants are the biggest issue, outsourcing the manufacturing function to a large outsourcer, which has economies of scale (we discuss outsourcing in the next section), might be a viable option.

- If the variable costs are the problem, an evaluation of procurement systems might be a good choice. If three suppliers supply the same type of products, it might be possible to reduce the number of suppliers and increase the quantity ordered from a single supplier. By doing so, bargaining power over suppliers is heightened and a better deal might be possible. Alternatively, alliances with other companies will increase the quantity and resulting power over suppliers.

- Experience effects are difficult to manage, as it takes time to accumulate experience. M&As or recruiting experienced people are potential ways to gain experience in a short time period or, put differently, skipping the actual learning steps. It is also possible to "reset" the degree of experience by introducing innovative technology or business systems, as Dell did.

3 Accordingly, large firms cannot simply sit and look down on small rivals. Large firms also need to understand their sources of economies of scale and pay attention to rivals' moves that may nullify a current cost advantage of the large firms.

As internet companies are becoming more and more popular, some consultants and managers argue that "large firms are dinosaurs," and that "speed is more important than scale." To some extent, this is true. However, scale is and continues to be a very powerful weapon. The effects and cost advantages are almost guaranteed. Moreover, scale is reinforcing (large → cost advantage → larger). The value of scale and the power of large companies should not be underestimated.

Vertical Integration and Outsourcing

Whether a company should conduct a particular activity or purchase it from others (outsource) is often called the "make or buy" decision. Outsourcing generally refers to delegating a particular activity that used to be done within a company to an external supplier. The antonym of outsourcing is vertical integration. Rather than using other companies for activities that are needed, some companies will do these activities themselves. When a company incorporates some of the activities that are closer to raw materials and thus backward from customers, that is called backward integration and the opposite move is called forward integration, as shown in Figure 3.5.

It is difficult for any company to be good at everything, particularly in auxiliary functions. Thus, outsourcing is very

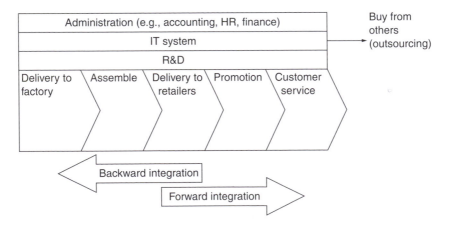

Figure 3.5 **Vertical integration and outsourcing.**

common in the areas of information technology systems and customer service. Partly because it is not economically viable to manage an information system department in house, many firms, even large firms such as P&G, outsource information systems to specialty companies such as IBM, EDS, and Accenture. Such companies (or parts of these companies) dedicate themselves to managing information technology, accumulating experiences, staying recent with technological development, and creating economies of scale (as many companies outsource to them). As a result, outsourcers can often provide better and less costly service to clients than an internal department could provide.

Outsourcing has many advantages, but it is also important to note the risks. Outsourcing a particular activity or a function when the function plays an important role for the success of the business is not a good idea. IBM made this outsourcing mistake when it invented the personal computer in 1981. IBM outsourced the two most important functions/parts: the microprocessor to Intel and the operating system to Microsoft. As a result, the PC became a commodity type of product very quickly. Almost anyone was able to enter the industry because there was no proprietary part. It was possible to buy a microprocessor and all other parts and assemble an "IBM compatible" PC. As a result, the PC became a very unprofitable business for IBM. IBM abandoned retail PC business in 1999, stopped manufacturing desktop PCs in 2002, and eventually exited from the PC business completely by selling its laptop business to Lenovo in 2004,[3] while both Intel and Microsoft have been extremely successful and profitable. Additionally, outsourcing a key function/part may result in overdependence on a supplier, creating such problems as limited power for price negotiation, shortage of the key part in the case that something happens to the supplier, and the threat of the forward integration (the supplier may become your competitor).

As another example, Xerox uses its own employees in the maintenance department to fix problems with copy machines and printers. Would it be better for a manufacturer whose expertise resides in technology to outsource such a localized and fragmented business function such as maintenance? Xerox did not do so because, in their view, after sales service and maintenance provides valuable information that is critical to improving products. Xerox felt outsourcing the maintenance would let outsourcers "leak" valuable information.[4] Maintenance is not one of Xerox's core strengths but maintenance also plays an important role for the success of Xerox. Another example is JP Morgan Chase. In 2004, it announced that it would bring back its technology functions outsourced to IBM in 2002. According to the *Wall Street Journal*, Jamie Dimon, COO at that time and current CEO of the company, made clear that "he thinks technology infrastructures can convey a competitive advantage."[5]

Like outsourcing, vertical integration also has benefits and risks. Jeans and other clothing companies used to delegate the sales function almost entirely to department stores and local stores. In fact, GAP started as a retailer of Levi's jeans in 1969. But we now see many stores owned by clothing companies including GAP, Limited, Zara, and H&M. Such integration is important when coordination across activities and functions plays a key role in the success of an organization. In the clothing business, brand image is critical. Even if you use high quality material and heavily promote a high-end image, a high quality brand may not be established if the actual products are sold at a bargain wagon with cheaper products. In this sense, vertical integration can contribute to securely controlling key functions. Moreover, it is difficult to predict which color or style will become "in style" in advance, yet companies want to minimize both opportunity loss and inventory costs. What clothing companies can do is to obtain information about which color/style is selling well as quickly as possible, pass the information to the factory, and make additional products that are sold well before a season ends.

Sharp, famous for its AQUOS high definition TV, used to be a second class manufacturer compared to Panasonic and Sony. Although Sharp manufactured high quality TVs, it did not manufacture the key device in the TV, the cathode-ray tube (CRT). As a result, retailers perceived Sharp as a second class manufacturer. Additionally, when Sharp entered China, it was initially very successful. However, soon local manufacturers started buying CRTs and other parts and built TVs with similar qualities as Sharp's. These experiences made the CEO decide to backward integrate and manufacture flat panels by itself. The decision was very risky as manufacturing flat panels required a huge investment, but the reward is enormous.[6]

Another often-cited benefit of integration can be achieved "by owning distribution channels such as stores (i.e., forward integration), saving on margins paid to distributors, and thus increasing profitability." However, in this case, a company needs to own the sales function and assets associated with it. As Figure 3.6 shows, a company should generate profits in response to the investment for the sales function. Otherwise, overall return-on-investment (ROI) or return-on-assets (ROA) decreases. To justify vertical integration, the integration must generate additional value (e.g., sales) that maintains or even increases ROI. In other words, as discussed in the examples of clothing companies, forward integration needs to have benefits beyond just saving margins paid to distributors.

Again, vertical integration has its own risks. An interesting example is the contrast between GM (or "the big three") and Toyota (or Japanese car manufacturers). At one time, GM manufactured most of the auto parts within the company, while Toyota used many suppliers (Keiretsu companies). It sounds

Figure 3.6 **Merit of vertical integration.**

logical for GM to make, not buy, parts because GM is large enough to enjoy economies of scale and coordination should be easier. But, vertical integration tends to result in a large and bureaucratic organization. Internal politics become intense. From a perspective of a particular parts department, a big customer is always there and products are guaranteed to be purchased, regardless of the quality. There will be limited incentive to be efficient or innovative. Even when better and inexpensive parts are available outside an organization, it is difficult to use an outside supplier.

Essentially, outsourcing and vertical integration are mirror-images of each other. The benefits of outsourcing are the risks of vertical integration and vice versa. It is fair to say that there is not a "no brainer" decision in terms of make or buy. A company has to understand the context, critically evaluate both pros and cons of outsourcing and vertical integration, and make a decision. If you think the decision is easy, most likely something is being missed.

	Outsourcing	Vertical integration
Benefits	• Hard to be better at everything (focus) • Flexibility (e.g., can use new technology/new supplier when it appears) • Less bureaucratic	• Coordination and control can be easier (including quick feedback) • Secure supply/scarce resources/ key technology/knowledge
Risks	• Possible loss of key resources/ competencies (may be absorbed by the third company) • Dependence on particular suppliers (loss of knowledge, little bargaining power, no competitive advantage) • Coordination costs may be higher	• Need capital • Bureaucracy (e.g., large size, "taken-it-for-granted" assembly division must use our parts regardless of quality) • Coordination costs/risks across divisions (capacity balance, assessment of contributions)

Figure 3.7 **Vertical integration vs. outsourcing.**

CORE CASE: SOUTHWEST AIRLINES

Southwest Airlines started its first flight in 1971, seven years before the Airline Deregulation Act was signed by Jimmy Carter in 1978. At that time, the overall environment of the airline industry could be described with the five forces framework as follows:

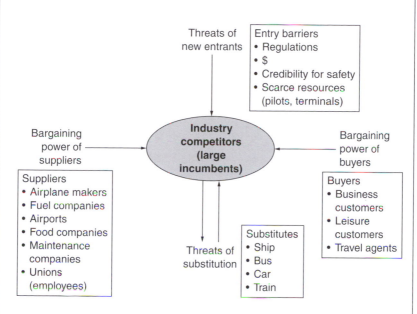

The airline business is heavily fixed-cost oriented and increasing the capacity utilization plays an important role in generating profits. At that time, many incumbent airlines used the "hub-and-spoke system," where customers who fly local airports first go to a major "hub" airport and fly to another hub or their final destination. By doing so, airlines can sum up the customers at hubs and maximize capacity utilization of the flights departing from the hubs. Meanwhile, Southwest took a "direct-flight system" from a local airport to another local airport without using a hub.

Southwest Airlines also implemented various practices to lower the costs of operations and passed the savings on to customers. Such practices included no food, no assigned seats, no travel agents, use of only one type of airplane (Boeing 737), use of less crowed local airports, and high turnaround of airplanes. The family culture, attributable to its founder, Herb Kelleher, contributed to the cooperation among employees for providing inexpensive yet friendly service to customers.

Although competitors have tried to imitate Southwest Airlines' business model and Southwest had some tough times (particularly after 9/11), Southwest continues to be one of the most successful airlines.

Sources: Southwest Airlines; Freberg, K. 1996. *Nuts! Southwest Airlines' crazy recipe for business and personal success*. Austin, TX: Bard Press; Porter, P.E. 1996. "What is strategy?" *Harvard Business Review*, November/December, 61–78. The five force framework is adapted with the permission of Free Press, a Division of Simon & Schuster, Inc., from Porter, E.M. 1980. *Competitive Strategy: Techniques for analyzing industries and competitors*. Copyright ©1980, 1998 by The Free Press. All rights reserved.

The success story of Southwest Airlines has been so famous that various articles and textbooks discuss its story. What can we learn from Southwest Airlines?

Entry Decision

Let's examine the external environment using the five forces framework when Southwest Airlines started its operation. The definition of the industry is straightforward in this case: airline industry.

Suppliers

It is important to be as systematic as possible in conducting analysis. In thinking suppliers, an income statement of a major player in the industry will be very helpful, as expenses are those that are paid to suppliers.

In the airline industry, suppliers include airplane makers, fuel companies, airports, food companies, and maintenance companies. It is important not to forget employees as they sometimes have very high bargaining power (particularly when unionized).

Buyers

In general, airline customers can be categorized into two types, business travelers who are concerned with schedules and leisure customers who are more sensitive to prices. Although travel agents should be categorized as suppliers from the perspective of expense, they can be categorized as buyers as they represent customers and act like a middle-man.

Substitutes

As discussed earlier, the distinction between competition and substitution is sometimes unclear and arbitrary. In this case, a ship, bus, car, and/or train can be substitutes to airline services. Also it is important to note that substitutes are not the only threats. If they can substitute us, we can substitute them. The relationship should be reciprocal, not one way.

New Entrants

The airline industry had very high entry barriers, particularly before 1978. Besides regulation, entry barriers included need for capital for airplanes, credibility for safety, and scarce assets typically taken by incumbents such as terminals and pilots.

Rivalry

The airline industry had many players already as of 1971, suggesting high competition and possible retaliation when new companies enter the industry.

At first glance, it is fair to say that the airline industry was not a very attractive industry to enter in 1971. Besides high entry barriers, there were many large incumbents, and suppliers included many powerful companies. The market seemed to be matured and thus competition could only increase. In fact, incumbents tried to block entry by suing Southwest.

Yet, Kelleher decided to enter. Why? This is a very good example in terms of *how to use analysis*, as opposed to *how to follow analysis*. Just because five forces analysis indicates unattractiveness of an industry, it does not mean that a company should give up. The industry at that time was full of inefficiencies and unmet needs that Southwest could take advantage of. In effect, the unattractiveness was pretty much dependent on the current rules of the industry. By operating more efficiently and decreasing the price of air travel, the market could grow and such "industry shifting rule changes" make it difficult for competitors to imitate Southwest's strategy.

Southwest's Strategy

Southwest focused on lowering its costs and passing the savings on to customers. To do so, Southwest did *everything*. It did not offer any food or reserved seats (which is called "no frills"). It did not use travel agents and saved fees. Only one type of airplane was used, which lowered the cost of pilot training, pilot scheduling, mechanic training, and maintenance (including parts inventory costs). By using direct flights with less crowded airports, it decreased turnaround time, leading to high airplane utilization. The cooperation among employees also contributed to lower costs through helping each other and lowering the number of people required to operate an airplane.

Such *consistency* toward lowering costs was seen not only across different activities but also across hierarchies. Kelleher showed his commitment to lower costs in a number of ways and at one time, he froze his salary to persuade pilots to freeze their salaries.

Although each of the cost saving activities was not difficult to imitate individually, the constellation of the activities were difficult to imitate. Many competitors imitated a number of activities that were easy for them to imitate, but failed to imitate the constellation of activities resulting in an inability to compete with Southwest. Subsidiaries of large airlines tended to use multiple airplanes their parents owned, leading to higher costs eventually. Some of them also could not terminate the relationships with travel agents.

Arguably, the most difficult thing for competitors to imitate was the culture of Southwest. Its family culture was an intangible resource that was developed over time. In the meantime, Southwest continued to strengthen the culture by selecting people who fit with the culture and providing intensive training. Moreover, Southwest took a risk of entering large airports such as Denver to continue to grow, a source of motivation and opportunity for employees.

Finally, it is important to note that such intangible resources such as motivation of employees and a family culture per se are not a competitive advantage. The intangible resources become a competitive advantage when such resources are actually used to provide better service or less costly service (with the same quality) to customers.

4
BUSINESS LEVEL STRATEGY

The previous three chapters have emphasized that strategy is a plan to win and discussed the importance of 3Cs (Customer, Competition, Company) in formulating strategy. In this chapter, we elaborate upon how to win. As repeatedly discussed in this text, the key of strategy is *differentiation* from competitors.

Business level strategy focuses on how to win in a single business. Many companies have multiple businesses, either because a particular business is matured or the resources and know-how developed in the business could be used elsewhere. As such, identifying fields of war or areas/businesses a company operates is also a crucial decision. We discuss how to identify such areas, allocate resources, and manage multiple businesses in Chapter 5, on corporate level strategy.

From the perspective of customers, which service/product they want to buy can be determined by the comparison of the attractiveness of each of the service/products offered by various suppliers. To measure the attractiveness, customers consider both value they obtain from the service/product and the price they pay for the service/product, which follows the simple formula below.

$$\text{Attractiveness} = \frac{\text{Value of the service/product}}{\text{Price of the service/product}}$$

Accordingly, there are two general business level strategies: one is lowering the denominator and increasing the attractiveness to customers. This is called a cost-leadership strategy, as a company lowers the cost and passes the savings on to consumers by offering a lower price for customers to pay for the service/product. The other is increasing the numerator and increasing the attractiveness to the customer. This is typically called a differentiation strategy. Note that this naming is a little misleading because a company following a cost-leadership strategy also differentiates itself by lowering costs. However, as the naming is so popular, we also use the term differentiation strategy to indicate the business level strategy of increasing the perceived value of a service/product and thus increasing the attractiveness of it to customers.

Of course, a company will be stronger if it can both increase the numerator and decrease the denominator. However, as we will discuss later, activities to increase the value are very different from activities to decrease costs. If a company attempts to pursue both, given the limitation of resources, it will likely end up stuck in the middle, and be neither low cost enough nor be differentiated enough to attract customers. Again, the importance of *trade-off* applies here as well.

There are three points to keep in mind. First, whether a cost-leadership strategy or differentiation strategy is pursued, it should not be forgotten that companies are competing. In other words, even if attractiveness of a service/product is increased drastically, if competitors do a little more, they will win. A service/product needs to be *more* attractive either by decreasing the price *more* or increasing the value *more than competitors.*

Second, a cost-leadership strategy is not necessarily equated with a low price strategy. Sometimes, advertising stresses the very low price of a particular product. Such promotions are often used to attract customers to the stores expecting the customers to buy more than the particular product that is on sale. This is a marketing tactic. A real cost-leadership strategy aims at developing a business model that structurally lowers the cost and passes the savings on to customers by lowering prices. One such example is Costco's wholesale model in which stores are less costly warehouses and products are sold in bulk.

Third, even if a cost-leadership strategy is pursued, it does not necessarily mean that the value of the service/product can be ignored. As the math formula suggests, it is important to provide a less costly service/product than competitors holding the value constant. Otherwise, the attractiveness calculated in the previous formula will not go up. Similarly, the costs and resulting price needs to be thought about even with a differentiation strategy.

It is useful to use the following two steps.

Step 1: Identify target customers. That is, are they those who are more concerned about price or value? Think about an example of an automobile. Some customers think of automobiles as a tool to move from A to B, while others want additional functions including the perceived prestige offered by a high quality brand.

Step 2: Increase the attractiveness of your service/product. If the target customers prefer basic functions, the goal is to provide such functions with lower costs than competitors. When target customers want unique features and additional frills, they need to be offered. However, even when targeting high-end segments, it is important to know that there are almost always competitors, as Mercedes competes with BMW and Lexus. If the cost of a product (i.e., price) is much higher than that of competitors, it may be difficult to justify a differentiation strategy. When both the numerator and denominator go up, attractiveness to the consumer may not go up enough to beat the competitors.

Cost-Leadership Strategy

A cost-leadership strategy can be defined as a strategy to lower the cost structurally more than competitors by doing something different from competitors or doing the same things as competitors in a different way and passing the savings on to customers by lowering the price.[1] There are many ways to do so "structurally" (e.g., in a sustainable way), as opposed to "opportunistically" (e.g., purchasing products from a supplier that went bankrupt and liquidates inventory). There are a few major ones: standardization, omission, and economies of scale.

1   Standardization: When just one type of product is offered as opposed to tens or hundreds (assuming the total quantity is equivalent), the cost of the product is much lower because (1) it increases the volume per part, resulting in economies of scale (see below), (2) different lines are not necessary and often times just one line can be used. A company cannot only save line-investment but also increase the utilization of the line, (3) costs of inventory become lower as many different parts for different types of products are not needed, and (4) training employees is simplified. As a result, the cost of labor can be decreased not only by lower training costs but also by hiring less-skilled workers.

   McDonald's is a good example. By limiting the number of menu items they offer, they maximize the utilization of the store and equipment in the store. As a result of a simplified menu, employees' activities are standardized and compartmentalized and they are easily replaceable. Southwest using only Boeing 737s is another example. It is also well known that the innovation of the Model T-Ford was spurred by Mr. Ford's insight about standardizing screws, which until then were customized one by one. Meanwhile, companies sometimes develop too many variations and increase costs drastically to try to differentiate.

2   Omission: It is possible to save costs by simply omitting functions that do not add much value to customers. Dell skipped retailers and passed the savings to customers. Similarly, Southwest omitted travel agents to lower its costs and resulting prices. Although this idea sounds obvious, we often observe companies that are haunted by conventional practices and take old needs for granted.

3   Economies of scale: As discussed in the previous chapter, economies of scale are a very powerful way to reduce

costs. In relation to standardization, using a large factory or line saves various administrative and overhead costs per unit in comparison with using a small factory. Experience can also be accumulated more rapidly. Increasing the quantity of orders will allow better deals to be negotiated from suppliers. To do so, the types of product and the number of suppliers will need to be reduced.

In relation to omission, outsourcing is another way to reduce costs by omitting a particular function within your value chain and taking advantage of the economies of scale of the outsourcers. An article reported that Wal-Mart demands suppliers to delegate the delivery to Wal-Mart (and lower the price of the products) so that Wal-Mart could take advantage of economies of scale and lower the cost of delivery and final products.[2]

Risks of Cost-Leadership Strategy

It is important to understand the risks of these activities. It is not unusual for auto manufacturers to use common parts across different car models (i.e., standardize parts). Sometimes, the ratio of common parts is so high that two supposedly different types of cars look identical. Such sister cars often fail due to loss of identity. Meanwhile, Chrysler tried to reduce costs by sharing parts with Daimler that refused to do so to maintain brand image.[3] Obviously, investing in a large factory is accompanied with the risks of overinvestment, change in technology, and changes in customer needs. Also low costs may not increase the attractiveness of the product when new technology fundamentally changes the product, as is often the case with mobile phones (e.g., from analog to digital to smart). Another risk of pursuing economies of scale is limiting the number of suppliers too much (i.e., one). By ordering from only one supplier, the order size is increased and thus a better deal should be expected. Meanwhile, it also means that a company is totally dependent on one supplier. When something happens to the supplier, it means trouble for the buyer.

Moreover, given an over-dependence on a single supplier, the supplier may exercise bargaining power and charge higher prices. Typically, companies have alternative sources of supply to avoid such risks.

There is an important but often mixed up distinction: *making a cheap product* vs. *making a product cheaply*. The latter is the cost-leadership strategy, not the former. It is not very difficult to make a cheap product by using low quality material and poorly trained workers. But, such products are unlikely to meet customers' needs. Even if they meet customers' needs, there will be always cheaper (and lower-quality) products. In this sense, making a cheap product is not a strategy. However, when companies are competing intensely and cost pressure is high, one may want to choose an easier alternative, which is "making a cheap product" as opposed to "making a product cheaply." Such seduction often results in poor product quality and loss of competitiveness.

Differentiation Strategy

Compared to a cost-leadership strategy, there are many options for pursuing a differentiation strategy, depending on the target customers. While cost is almost a universal concern for customers, value can be very different customer by customer. In other words, identifying target customers and their needs is probably the most important step in pursuing a differentiation strategy. Yet, the importance of doing something different from competitors or doing the same things in a different way from competitors still applies. To the particular targeted customers, a company wants to develop a strategy providing a more attractive service/product than competitors in a way competitors cannot easily imitate.

Generally, there are two types of "value":

1   functional value (i.e., additional function, higher quality, higher speed);
2   emotional value (i.e., brand image, prestige).

To increase functional value, a company needs to invest in R&D so that it can get new and innovative technologies. It will take some time to establish a certain brand (i.e., emotional value). Accordingly, in addition to investment on promotion, a company may want to consider alliances with other companies or individuals that already have a prestigious brand or image.

Risks of Differentiation Strategy

Similar to a cost-leadership strategy, a differentiation strategy also has some risks. First, investment in R&D does not guarantee that innovative technology and products/services will be developed. If competitors find a better technology, an investment can be wasted. Second, value is always evaluated from the perspective of customers, not from the perspective of a technology expert. Even if value is added theoretically through a better function or technology, customers may not be impressed enough to pay a premium for the function. We saw this in the video game industry. Sony's Playstation 3 is more advanced in terms of technology than Nintendo's Wii. The Wii, however, attracted many more customers. Finally, customer segments need to be carefully identified. The narrower a target segment, the easier it is for a company to differentiate itself, as they can focus on the very specific needs of a certain customer segment. However, the customer segment may be too narrow and too small to recoup investment, unless a very high price is charged such as Ferrari does.

As a cost-leadership strategy needs continuous efforts to lower costs, a differentiation strategy is also not a one-time deal. Imitators need to be expected, thus, it is important to continue to be distinct. Continuous investment in technology is certainly important. Replacing products or technology with a company's own new products often stimulates debates within a company (i.e., cannibalization). In the current competitive environment, it is probably reasonable to assume that unless a company cannibalizes itself, someone else will.[4] Once a brand is established, it is important not to dilute the image. In relation to vertical integration discussed in the previous chapter, many high-end brand companies control distribution very tightly either by being vertically integrated or by selecting very limited high quality distributors.

First-Mover Advantages

To obtain customers, it is important to provide a more attractive service/product than competitors by either lowering costs more than competitors or by increasing the value more than competitors. This section discusses the ability to develop such a structural difference from competitors from a perspective of time. More specifically, first-mover advantages and second-mover advantages (or first-mover disadvantages) are discussed.

Being the first company to provide a particular service/product can generally lead to various advantages over second or late movers. The advantages include:

* technological leadership (e.g., patent, accumulated knowledge);
* preemption of scarce assets (e.g., location, inputs, skilled workers);
* switching costs (e.g., brand loyalty, contracts/relationship);
* cost advantages (e.g., investment to fend off competitors, learning).

A good example is Amazon.com's advantages as an online retailer. Because of its early investments and exposure, most people think of Amazon first when they think about buying something online. Moreover, Amazon accumulated knowledge and experience through which it developed very sophisticated logistics systems and customer management systems to promote products. Prius from Toyota is another good example. By being the first hybrid car on the market, Prius established a dominant brand image as a legitimate hybrid car. Moreover, Toyota accumulated knowledge and feedback on how to improve the Prius and expanded this technological advantage over competitors.

However, as we discussed a number of times already, every strategy has risks. Sometimes, being the second mover or second company in the market can be more advantageous. Such second-mover advantages (first-mover disadvantages) can be described below as:

- free-ride on first-mover investments;
- resolution of technological or market uncertainty.

Being the first company means, by definition, customers have never experienced the type of service/product provided. Moreover, nobody knows whether customers will actually like the product/service. In other words, first movers have to educate customers under uncertainty. In the case of Amazon, it made a tremendous investment, as people were not very comfortable using their credit cards for online shopping. Amazon had to spend a lot of money to promote not only their business per se but also safety issues for using credit cards for online purchases. Once a first mover has made initial investments to educate customers, second and late movers often do not have to spend money educating consumers. They free-ride the first mover's investments and efforts. Moreover, first movers can provide a good model from which a second mover can learn from. That is a first mover provides a road map for what works and what will not work. By being a second mover, a company may be able to develop better or less expensive services/products than the first mover as Microsoft did to outperform Netscape.

It should be noted that Amazon.com was not the first mover in terms of internet retail business. There were others. However, the "real" first movers failed before obtaining any first-mover advantages. In fact, many Wall Street analysts were very skeptical of the survival of Amazon at one point[5] (my favorite joke at that time is that Amazon should change its

domain name to Amazon.org – as it was a non-profit organization). First movers need to keep investing until it is perceived as
a first mover, although eventual success is not guaranteed.

Many students point out that being a first mover is good
because there are no competitors. Starting a new business by
exploring unmet customer needs sounds promising. However, it is possible that there are no competitors because
there are no needs or it is not economically viable to meet
the needs. In this sense, being a first mover is a high-risk
high-return move. One such example was Webvan.com, which
tried to sell groceries over the internet but went bankrupt in
2001. Various players that provided similar services started
after the failure of Webvan, which provided various important lessons.[6]

Finally, being a successful first mover does not mean that a
firm will be successful for a long time. Customer needs and
technology change. Competitors learn to imitate successful
business models and products. First movers need to continue
to strengthen their advantages, as second and late movers will
always have an opportunity to take over the leading position
of the industry. Whether companies take cost-leadership strategies or differentiation strategies, they have to have long-term
success in mind and continue to improve or even replace the
current business model to maintain their competitive advantages over competitors in the long run.

CORE CASE: STARBUCKS CORPORATION

Starbucks Corporation was formerly originated by three entrepreneurs in 1971. In 1983, a year after he joined Starbucks, Howard Schulz visited Italy and was impressed with the atmosphere coffee could create. Convinced that American people could enjoy such a romantic experience through coffee, he persuaded the founders to expand and eventually purchased Starbucks in 1987.

Understanding that "There is no secret sauce here. Anyone can do it," Schulz expanded Starbucks aggressively. In doing so, he did not use franchising. Instead, the company owned most of the shops and expanded city by city, first completely dominating one city then moving to another city. Using the information of the mail order business, Schulz identified potential areas that had strong needs for the premium coffee and expanded from Seattle to Chicago in 1987, Los Angeles in 1991, and to the District of Columbia in 1993. In just ten years, Starbucks increased its number of stores from 17 to 1412.

Growth of Starbucks stores

Year	1987	1988	1989	1990	1991	1992	1993	1994	1995	1996	1997
# of stores	17	33	55	84	116	165	272	425	676	1015	1412

To provide not only a high quality coffee but also a high quality experience, Schulz used the finest beans, from roasting all the way to serving coffee to customers. To encourage employees to be partners in this new business and educate US customers who had been satisfied with low quality coffee for a long time, Shultz invested heavily in employee training, benefits, and even stock option plans called the Bean Stock plan. "[Our] part-timers are on the front line with our customers. If we treat them right, we feel they will treat (customers) right," says a Vice President of the company.

Sources: Starbucks, Starbucks Corporation (Schilling, M., and Kotha, S. University of Washington).

Starbucks is a great example of an entrepreneur that successfully created a new market. Before Schulz started, most US customers had been satisfied with low quality coffee. Although the gourmet coffee market was growing, the market size was very small. Along with increasing heath consciousness, the coffee business in the US was regarded as matured and having no bright future. If he had analyzed the industry with the five forces framework first, it is questionable if he would have really entered the business.

Instead, his enthusiasm for this business was born with his inspiration obtained when he visited Italy. Maybe he did analyze the industry and found out that the gourmet segment was increasing, but such a story can only be ad hoc justification. It does not mean that analysis is unimportant. Yet, it is important to point out the fact that Schultz first came up with a hypothesis that US people could enjoy high quality coffee in a nice setting. This story re-emphasizes that industry analysis provides information with which you make a decision, not conclusion itself.

His growth strategy focused on being a first mover. By doing so, Starbucks enjoyed customer loyalty, a strong established brand, and secured good locations. It is important to note that Starbucks did not simply expand without any concern for the risks involved in being the first mover. The beauty of the strategy was minimizing the risks of being the first mover by using the information from the mail order business to expand city by city. It would be a tremendous investment to educate all US customers simultaneously. It is possible that second and late movers might have imitated and taken over Starbucks. To avoid such problems, Starbucks took a strategy of dominating a city before moving to another city. By doing so, Starbucks not only saved on investments in educating customers, but also took advantage of word of mouth, and minimized the chance of copy-cats eroding Starbucks' turfs. In fact, competitors such as Seattle's Best Coffee (SBC) aggressively took advantage of being a second mover. It waited for Starbucks to open stores and educate customers in a particular area, then found a franchisee to open a new store near the Starbucks.

Another important point is the *consistency*. Starbucks did *everything* to provide the "Starbucks experience." It used the highest quality beans, highly vertically integrated systems, and trained and motivated employees, most of them part-timers. Arguably, the most important component of their business model was *not* using franchising. Although franchising is less costly, particularly when a company wants to grow rapidly, Schultz stuck to owning stores. Given that the "Starbucks experience" involves both high quality coffee and high quality customer service, it was absolutely necessary for Starbucks to impose a very high standard in both. Such consistent and uncompromising emphasis on value differentiated Starbucks from other competitors (SBC was acquired by Starbucks in 2003).

As of 2006, Starbucks owned about 9000 stores in the US (12,500 stores worldwide). According to an article in the *Wall Street Journal* (October 24, 2006), the proportion of take-out and drive-through sales in the US is approaching 80% of total sales. Given that the value Starbucks had focused on was the "experience," this number clearly suggests that the market has changed as Starbucks proliferated. Moreover, in 2007, it was reported that Schulz sent a memo among executives questioning whether Starbucks commoditize its brand for the sake of growth (*Wall Street Journal*, February 24, 2007). In 2009, Starbucks surprised customers and competitors by announcing it would sell instant coffee, called Via.

The struggle of Starbucks also suggests that a strategy needs to be continuously renewed. Being a successful first mover does not guarantee long-term success, as both markets and competition change. Once a market leader feels comfortable with a current strategy, a long-term decline starts.

5

CORPORATE LEVEL
STRATEGY

Most businesses have a life cycle: inception, growth, and maturity. Due to technological change, maturity of markets, or the availability of substitutes, at some point current businesses no longer have a bright future. As discussed in Chapter 2, growth is almost always important for management. A company working on a matured business needs to find other businesses and opportunities to continue to grow. Entering new businesses while managing current businesses and/or managing multiple businesses is considered corporate level strategy, which is typically called diversification.

Depending on how diversification is managed, companies competing with similar strategies in the same industry at one point often turn out to be very different in the long run. Thirty years ago, Cannon, Nikon, and Minolta were all famous camera manufacturers. It was Minolta that launched the world's first auto-focus single-lens reflex (SLR) camera in 1985. Today, Cannon has a strong presence in office copiers and printers and Nikon has a major presence in precision equipment and instruments such as equipment for semiconductor manufacturing, although both of them still manufacture cameras (mostly digital cameras). Minolta, however, merged with a 35 mm photo film company called Konica in 2003, sold its camera business to Sony in 2006, and now is struggling to catch up with Cannon whose sales are now about four times as large as that of Konica-Minolta and whose profits are five times as large.

Diversification

Corporate level strategy is concerned with which businesses, if any, a company should enter and how to manage those businesses. From a perspective of shareholders, it is not necessarily important for a company to diversify, as shareholders can diversify by owning stocks of different types of companies. Besides growth, top management needs to show that the company's diversification is creating value, which is "synergy." Suppose that company X enters a new business by acquiring an existing company Y. Think about the new company Z as a combination of X and Y. There will be three scenarios:

1   the value of Z < the value of X + the value of Y;
2   the value of Z = the value of X + the value of Y;
3   the value of Z > the value of X + the value of Y.

If the result of the diversification is either 1 or 2, shareholders will be very unhappy. There is no reason for company X to diversify if the result of such a diversification is a decrease or no change in overall value. In other words, with diversification, the goal is to create a company whose value is more than the sum of each of the previous individual businesses.

In general, diversification is planned with the framework shown in Figure 5.1. The x-axis indicates whether the current product/technology can be utilized or not and the y-axis indicates whether the service/product can be sold to existing customers or new customers.

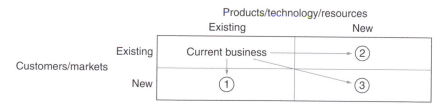

Figure 5.1 **A framework in considering diversification.**

Some companies enter new markets by utilizing existing products/technologies/resources ①. Using the example of the camera manufacturers, they used their photographic technologies developed through their camera businesses (to consumers) to enter copying businesses and precision equipment businesses (mainly business customers). Another example can be seen in Amazon.com. Initially, Amazon focused on books and CDs. After Amazon learned and developed sophisticated systems for marketing, sales, customer management, and distribution, Amazon started diversifying products including cosmetics, stationeries, kitchen goods, consumer electronics, and PCs which allowed them to use a current business model and technology and resources to target wider customer segments.

Another way of diversifying is selling new products to existing customers ②. A classic example is what is called "one-stop shopping." Sears diversified their businesses into real estate brokerage, insurance, and banking so that Sears could sell additional products/services to existing customers who regularly visited the store to shop for clothes, electronics, and appliances. Financial firms also diversified by trying to sell their current customers as many products as possible, such as checking and savings accounts, mutual funds, and brokerage of stocks and bonds. The Superstore concept of Wal-Mart and Target, which added groceries to traditional stores, is another example diversifying by selling more products to current customers.

Sometimes, companies enter a new market unrelated to current businesses ③. A famous example is Seagram's (the Canadian whiskey maker) entry into the entertainment business in 1995 by a grandson of its founder, Edgar Bronfman, Jr. Sony's entry into the movie business in 1989 can also be included in this category. Sony had very limited knowledge about the movie business and arguably was abused by the industry moguls.[1] In the 1970s, this type of diversification was quite popular and there were many conglomerates that owned totally different businesses under one umbrella corporation. The International Telephone and Telegraph Company (ITT) led by Harold

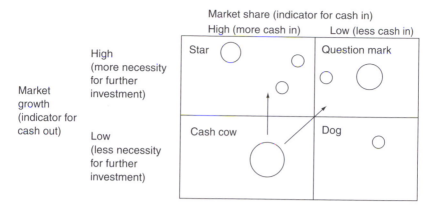

Figure 5.2 **BCG matrix.**

Note
Each circle indicates a business with the size of the circle indicating the sales; the arrow indicates the direction of investment.

Green increased its earnings 58 consecutive quarters through its bread business (Continental Baking), car rental (Avis), insurance (Harford), and hotel chains (Sheraton Hotels).[2] Accordingly, at that time, a diversification strategy was equated with resource allocation within the company. The BCG matrix (Figure 5.2) that categorizes businesses into four types (cash cow, star, question mark, and dog) and showed in and out of the cash flow across those businesses was very popular.

Synergy Effects

As pointed out earlier, diversification cannot be justified unless the value of the whole is more than the sum of each of the businesses. The difference between the whole and sum of each of the businesses is referred to as "synergy."

One way to develop synergy is economies of scope, which refers to the efficient usage of common resources for multiple purposes. While economies of scale contribute to lower costs by doing the same thing in a large scale, economies of scope increases efficiency by doing different things with the same resources. The Superstore concept is one example of using the same resources (store, brand name) for different purposes (selling groceries in addition to TVs and toys). Gas stations also enjoy economies of scope by selling both gas and other small goods.

In relation, various companies diversify by utilizing existing resources, hoping to be more efficient than competitors. Unfortunately, such diversification does not always work well. Toyota entered the home building business a long time ago, hoping to utilize its manufacturing technology, brand name, and dealer network for the home business. After more than 30 years, the division is still small and not very profitable. Ford's entry into the insurance business and junk yard business was based on a similar idea. Ford knows the auto business. Car insurance and junk yards are related to the auto business, thus they should be able to develop a synergy and succeed. Unfortunately Ford's insurance and junk yard businesses were terminated after Jack Nasser was fired in 2001.[3]

Many failures can be identified from companies trying to follow a one-stop shopping strategy. Besides Sears, AT&T also provides an interesting example. As a local and long-distance telephone service company, it offered "bundling" packages of cell phone service to its customers. For unknown reasons, AT&T also offered free oil changes to local and long-distance telephone service customers. What customers chose was not the cell phone service, which AT&T believed was a logical choice. Instead, customers of local and long-distance services wanted free oil changes from AT&T.[4] It should be convenient for customers to purchase related services from one supplier. Moreover, from the perspective of a supplier, providing multiple services leads to closer relationships with customers and increases the switching costs of the customers. However, customers do not behave that way in many cases. Particularly, when the "packaged" products include both good ones and so-so or average ones, customers want to purchase good ones in each product category. The failure of the one-stop shopping idea often indicates rather self-centered thinking of suppliers, who ignored the real needs of customers.

Why Does Diversification (Entry to a New Business) Often Fail?

Although it is not surprising that the one-stop shopping idea that ignored customers' needs often failed, there are many other failures in companies' diversification initiatives. Why does diversification often result in failure? It is particularly puzzling when a company enters a market where the resources developed in the main business, business skills, assets, or relationships with customers, should be easily utilized.

There are a couple of common reasons why diversification often fails. First, a company often enters a new business without much commitment. A new business is, by definition, new to the company. It should not be surprising when companies are initially unsuccessful in doing something they have never done before. Patience and trial and error is important. Surprisingly, many companies expect to be successful with new businesses from the beginning. When the new business encounters a problem or two, people within its main business often criticize, with such comment as, "why do we have to spend money we made on such an unprofitable business?" Developing a new business is like raising a child. Investment is needed first. Unfortunately, companies often give up on businesses even before they reach adolescence.

In relation, it is relatively rare for a company to send top performers to new businesses. In many cases, top management retains high performing managers for the large and profitable (but matured) main businesses. Lower performing managers or managers with less potential are sent to operate new businesses. How can top management expect a new business inherently involving various challenges to be successful without sending top class managers and employees?

Finally, "sharing resources" is easier said than done. Two types of sharing resources are common: transferring intangible resources and sharing tangible resources. Transferable intangible resources include such things as brand name, knowledge, relationships with customers, or even a high credit rating. Because intangible resources do not depreciate when a new business uses them, transferring resources is relatively easy as seen in the example with different types of Oreos. GE also utilizes its high credit rating among various business units. Obviously, intangible resources can tarnish when they are abused. For example, a prestigious brand can be used to increase the image of a particular product. Meanwhile, such a prestigious brand image can be tainted when the quality of the product is poor.

Sharing tangible resources is more difficult. Although sharing common resources (i.e., economies of scope) makes sense, sharing essentially leads to dividing. Suppose a sales person who used to sell product X also needs to sell Y. Before, the person spent 100% of the time trying to sell X. When product Y comes from a new business, top management may want the sales person to spend more time pushing Y, which may result in the manager in charge of X not being happy. Such internal conflicts are common when tangible resources are shared among multiple products or departments.

How Can We Make Diversification (Entry to a New Business) Successful?

Professor Costas at the London Business School has elaborated on critical key success factors for diversification.[5]

First, existing resources are important, but to be successful in a new business, a company needs to think about whether the resources are superior to that of competitors as opposed to whether they have certain resources. Again business involves competition. Just because a company has some resources, success is not guaranteed.

Second, to be successful in a new business, a company needs to have *every* resource required to win the customers while competing with rivals. Even if a company has *some or most of the necessary* resources, they are unlikely to be successful if they lack a few key resources.

From the perspective of a diversifying company, a new business entered is something additional. However, from the perspective of the rivals within the industry of the new business, it is their core. It is reasonable to enter a new business to utilize slack resources, but such companies need to be as serious as the companies whose fate depends on the focal business. It is a war. Those who are more serious and more committed are likely to win.

Diversification should not be considered a tool to utilize existing resources. A new business is business. At the end of the day, a company needs to differentiate itself from competitors in the industry either through lower costs or higher value from the perspective of customers, whether it is a core business or a new business. Utilizing the existing resources is just one factor to formulate a strategy.

Practical Perspective Toward Diversification

Unless synergy is developed, diversification cannot be justified. Meanwhile, it is actually difficult to realize synergy. In fact, synergy is often used as a buzzword to defend an "unreasonable" diversification action such as entry into an unrelated business (e.g., Seagram's entry to an entertainment business) or for paying a very high price for an acquisition. In the case of eBay's acquisition of Skype in 2005 with $2.6 billion, Meg Whitman, CEO of eBay at that time, provided various justifications why it made sense for eBay to acquire Skype. One such justification was "it allows us to create this unique e-commerce engine for buyers and sellers around the world."[6] In 2007, eBay wrote down $1.4 billion for the acquisition. In 2010, eBay with its new CEO John Donahoe announced that it was selling Skype to a group of investors for $1.9 billion, because "the telecommunications software didn't fit well within the company's core business of connecting buyers and sellers."[7]

It may be more practical not to rely on uncertain synergy (i.e., synergy in sales) too much. In fact, failures of major acquisitions (e.g., Daimler and Chrysler, AOL and Time Warner) can be attributed to overly optimistic estimates of synergy such as economies of scope and joint-product development. Researchers and consultants warn that more certain synergy in cost saving such as reduction of redundant overhead may be a major source of value created by the diversification.

Some companies diversify without expecting any synergies from sales or cost cutting. For example, with GE all that is expected is a good credit rating from existing businesses. Arguing that "a combination of weak businesses only results in a weak company," GE Capital expects each of its businesses to be strong independently. By having multiple strong businesses, the rating of the company will remain high, which trickles down and benefits each business.[8]

To make diversification successful in the long run, top management needs to take various possibilities and contingency plans into consideration at the time of the initial decision. First, new businesses will always encounter various problems. A company needs to invest in people, time, and money to take care of problems. Second, new business may fail or the decision may turn out to be wrong after an investment is made. While it is beautiful to be successful after overcoming a number of problems and challenges, it is well known that managers and organizations often escalate their commitment to a losing project and waste a large amount of money by not being able to stop earlier.[9] To avoid such scenarios, it is desirable to set a target for withdrawal. Finally, failure per se may not necessarily be bad as long as managers and organizations learn from the failure and use the lessons learned for their next initiatives. In this sense, don't believe that an entry into a new business succeeds and be caught in surprise when it turns out to be a failure. Instead, managers can be prepared for failure and attempt to learn from it. Cannon experienced various failures and withdrawals but "technologies were accumulated and used for the next projects" (Fujio Mitarai, Chairman).[10] Finally, expecting synergy is one thing, but realizing the synergy is another. It is important to be as practical as possible when diversifying, as overly optimistic synergy stories can always be added after a diversification decision is made.

CORE CASE: GATEWAY

Founded in 1985 by Ted Waitt, Gateway (initially named Gateway 2000) grew rapidly using the direct model similar to Dell. While Dell continues to be a top PC manufacturer, Gateway dropped the ball and was eventually acquired by the Taiwanese company Acer in 2007. What happened?

Gateway had been famous for its low price products and good customer service. As the company went public in 1993 and grew further, investors and analysts argued that Gateway needed professional managers. In 1999, Waitt invited Jeff Weitzen (from AT&T) who imposed various rules and disciplines (e.g., call from a customer needs to be taken care of within 13 minutes).

At that time, most managers and analysts in the industry believed that the PC market would mature sooner rather than later, resulting in price competition. Along with the proliferation of the internet, Capellas (CEO of Compaq) and Weitzen both argued that they needed to shift their focus from PCs to software, internet-related peripherals, and services which bring higher profit margins, while Dell continued to stress the importance of the PC. Gateway also opened about 300 physical stores which not only provided services (e.g., training), but also was a way of penetrating the small-to-medium size company market. Such moves at Gateway were part of the "beyond the box strategy."

The strategy was a total failure. Investment in stores pushed the overhead cost of Gateway up about 40% in one year, reaching about twice that of Dell. Pursuing "disciplined and efficient" sales activities resulted in less customer satisfaction. Word of mouth sales went down dramatically.

In 2001, Ted Waitt fired Weitzen and came back as CEO. He took a "back to basic" strategy and emphasized the PC and closed the physical stores. However, the cost disadvantage over Dell was too large to catch up. Then, Gateway started selling high-margin consumer electronics such as large size TVs and digital cameras. In 2004, Gateway acquired the low-cost PC manufacturer e-Machines to fill the cost disadvantage over Dell as well as strengthen their relationship with retailers.

In six months, the new CEO Wayne Inoue (former CEO of e-Machines) announced that Gateway would again move back to the PC business by withdrawing from other electronics, which had about a quarter of the total Gateway sales. In 2006, Inoue was fired due to poor performance. After several unsuccessful trials to recover, Gateway agreed to be purchased by Acer in 2007.

Sources: "Please don't call us PC" *Fortune*, October 16, 2000; "I built this company, I can save it" *Fortune,* April 30, 2001; "Acer buys Gateway, bulks up for global fight" *Wall Street Journal*, August 28, 2007.

The failure of Gateway's diversification (beyond the box strategy) provides several important lessons.

Is a Market Matured?

In many cases, the decision to diversify is driven by the assessment that a current market/business is matured. In a matured market, a company's only alternative to grow is to attract customers from rivals, which often results in price competition and a decrease in margins. Thus, it makes sense to enter a new and higher margin business.

However, given the risks associated with entering a new business, top management should ask twice whether a market is really matured. In fact, several industries that were called matured at one point were able to regain growth, such as the TV industry and the coffee shop industry. In other words, market maturity is not given. Companies can stimulate a market by offering more attractive or innovative products/services. A market can evolve.

Resources and Trade-Off

Gateway had an important resource to diversify: relationships with customers. Additionally, they had sales reps, PCs, and all the resources that were needed to pursue diversification to offer services. The problem was trade-off. Gateway established its leading position in the PC industry with its low-cost business model which passed the savings on to customers. By diversifying, they attempted to offer high-margin services, Gateway shifted its focus from low-cost to services that required various investments which not only made total costs go up but also made its core PC business model weak. As a corporation, it was not clear whether it was pursuing a low-cost strategy or a differentiation strategy. Gateway was "stuck-in-the-middle." From the perspective of customers, products/services became less attractive. Unless it offered a PC that was attractive, customers would not visit Gateway in the first place.

The same resources (e.g., sales reps, stores) could be shared both for selling PCs and services. The issue of trade-off and consistency was somehow forgotten in pursuing diversification.

This trade-off problem shows the difficulty in successfully enjoying economies of scope.

Strengths

Although the problems are often attributed to Weitzen's "AT&Tnization of Gateway," the more fundamental problem was in its strategy. To repeat, the key of strategy is using strengths to provide better or cheaper services/products than competitors. The strengths that should have been used by Gateway were its low-cost and yet very friendly sales and customer services. In the process of shifting its focus to services, Weitzen emphasized too much on efficiency without thinking about the value of the sales and customer service functions for Gateway (and its customers). Rather than investing in the contacts with customers to strengthen the relationships with customers, the "beyond-the-box strategy" used the contacts as a convenient tool to push high-margin products, which made customers unsatisfied, and tarnished the value of the whole organization.

Ted Waitt tried to take Gateway back to its origin and refocused on the PC with high quality sales and customer service. However, once the strengths were lost, it was very difficult to regain. Without its uniqueness, Gateway had to go back and forth to find its next strategy. Such zigzagging is not uncommon. In fact, its rival Dell fired Kevin Rollins in 2007 and Michael Dell returned as CEO. Apple also experienced similar soul searching in the 1990s when it had four different CEOs. The bottom line: regardless of whether it is business level or corporate level, strategy should be based on the strengths of a company and thus needs trade-offs. Otherwise, the company will not be able to differentiate itself from competitors. Once such strengths were lost, the company essentially lost its identity. While it is important to continue to grow by diversifying into new businesses when current businesses are approaching a matured stage, top managers should not forget about the strengths and identity of the company.

6

M&As, ALLIANCE, AND INTERNATIONAL STRATEGY

So far, we have discussed key concepts in strategic management: 3Cs, analyses of external and internal environments, business level strategy, and corporate level strategy. Along these concepts, we stressed the importance of differentiation and trade-offs in thinking of strategy to provide more attractive products/services to target customers than competitors. In this chapter, we discuss specific strategic actions, mergers and acquisitions (M&As), alliances, and international strategy, which can all be part of business level strategies or corporate level strategies.

M&As and alliances with other companies have become one of the most important strategic tools for many organizations. For example, the total deal amount of M&As worldwide in 2006 was about $3.8 trillion, which is much larger than the $3.4 billion in 2000 at the peak of the internet bubble, twice as large as that of ten years ago, and about 20 times as large as that of a ten-year total from the decade of the 1980s.[1] Although the Lehman shock and the following economic slump decreased such activities, mass media continues to report M&As and alliances every day.

The recent battle between Dell and HP is a good example. To strengthen its service business, HP announced its acquisition of EDS with $13.9 billion on May 18, 2008. About a year later, Dell decided to acquire Perot Systems that Ross Perot, the founder of EDS, developed, with $3.9 billion, which was about a 65% premium over the traded stock price. The *Wall Street*

Journal reported the following comment from a consultant familiar with the deal, "If they'd been out ahead of this thing, they probably wouldn't be paying a high price, and they might not be buying Perot."[2] In 2010, HP and Dell fought over the data storage firm 3PAR. The stock of 3PAR traded at less than $10 before Dell's announcement of its intent to acquire 3PAR on August 16. The initial offer was $1.1 billion, about $17 per share. The bid heated up. HP eventually sealed the deal with $2.1 billion, or $33 a share.[3]

M&As

Objectives and Risks of M&As

Why do companies engage in mergers and acquisitions? Obviously, there are funds and investment banks that purchase distressed companies, clean them up, and sell them for a premium. But this section focuses on the strategic objectives of M&As.

The most popular objective of M&As is *buying important resources, including scale and speed.* In the case of Dell and HP, they acquired IT service companies that owned the know-how (typically within employees), reputation, and relationships with customers. It would not only be difficult but also time consuming to develop such resources from scratch. Although many of the tangible resources (e.g., computers and software) can be purchased, intangible resources are hard to obtain in a short time period. Speed is particularly important when trying to capture opportunities in a growing market. At a time when such resources are eventually developed, existing companies are likely to take all customers and build strong relationships with these customers (i.e., raising switching costs).

Motives behind M&As also include economies of scale that provide cost advantages and larger pockets that can be used for product development (particularly when rivals initiate M&As and increase scale). Given the risks associated with developing a new and hopefully blockbuster product in such industries as pharmaceuticals and computer games, it is understandable for large companies to acquire small companies that have promising ideas and products.

In relation to the corporate level strategy discussed in the previous chapter, it is important to note that M&As should be justified from the perspective of shareholders. More specifically, acquiring companies need to realize synergy by acquiring the target company. If the value of the total company is equal or even less than the sum of the acquirer value and the target value, shareholders can simply buy the stock of the two companies. In the context of M&As, such synergy is called *private synergy*.

Private synergy refers to a value derived from the acquisition of a target due to a unique set of resources that are complementary only between the two companies and not available among other bidders for the target. To acquire a certain company, an acquiring company will pay more than other bidders. Why can the acquirer pay more than others? The difference is the private synergy only the particular acquirer can enjoy. In other words, it is important to critically evaluate the size of the potential private synergy when pursuing an acquisition (in the previous chapter, it was emphasized that diversification often fails due to overly optimistic expectations for synergy). In M&As, it is possible the price of the target will go up dramatically when rivals compete with each other for a target company like an auction. The acquisition war between Dell and HP over 3PAR Inc., is a good example.[4] At this point, it is difficult to say which company is the real winner, HP or Dell (the shareholders of 3PAR are certainly the winner). If a company acquires a target company just to outbid rivals without private synergy, the acquisition is unlikely to increase shareholders' value.

Risks of M&As

As every strategy involves some risks, so do M&As. The risks are in many cases hand-in-hand with benefits.

M&As aim at achieving private synergy by acquiring important resources from the target company. As discussed in the previous chapter, synergy is easy to discuss but hard to realize. In the context of M&As, sharing and/or transferring knowledge and know-how often encounters various problems. The major source of the problems is the difference in company cultures, including the differences in how to communicate with each other. Because such intangible resources as know-how, knowledge, and even relationships with customers, are not necessarily stored in the target company, but rather are located within the employees of the company, such resources may be gone when key employees leave during or after the acquisition.

Another problem is the inherent difficulty in evaluating the target company's value, particularly when the value of the synergy involves intangible resources. Overly optimistic expectations of potential synergy often lead to excessive payments for target companies. An excessive payment may never be recouped even when some synergy is realized. It is often pointed out that top managers become obsessed with acquisition per se in competing with rivals (e.g., Dell vs. HP). M&As are a means to obtain resources, increase competitiveness, and achieve superior performance in the long run. Moreover, an acquisition is only a start, not an end. Once a target company is acquired, top managers need to work very hard to integrate the company so that actual synergy is realized. When M&As become a goal in a tough and often visible process of negotiation, not a means to increase the value of the focal company, the M&A is unlikely to be beneficial to the acquirer.

Thus, it is not easy to achieve a successful result through large M&As. Instead, acquisitions often result in the subsequent divestiture of the acquired company, with a large discount. Besides the well-known case of Daimler and Chrysler, which will be explained later, the *Wall Street Journal* (1999) reported notable examples of big flops.

Additionally, it is important to note that investment bankers such as Goldman Sacks and Morgan Stanley often play a very

Table 6.1 Examples of major acquisition failures

Acquirer	Target	Purchase year, price	Sales year, price	Lost value (proportion of the purchase price)
AT&T	NCR	1991 $7.4 billion	1994 $3.4 billion	$4.0 billion (54%)
Novel	Word Perfect	1994 $1.4 billion	1996 $124 million	$1.28 billion (91%)
Smith-Kline Beecham	Diversified Pharmaceutical	1994 $2.3 billion	1999 $700 million (plus $300 million tax saving)	$1.3 billion after tax saving (57%)
Eli-Lilly	PCS Health Systems	1994 $4.0 billion	1998 $1.5 billion	$2.5 billion (63%)
Quaker Oats	Snapple	1994 $1.7 billion	1997 $300 million	$1.4 billion (82%)

Source: *Wall Street Journal*, December 8, 1999.

important role in the M&As process. They take the role of the professional in engineering the acquisition from the financial perspective. Meanwhile, their fees ultimately depend on the deal amount. Because many companies do not engage in M&As very often, it is very difficult to evaluate and select the "right advisor." Instead, companies tend to pick investment banks based on their visibility.[5] While finding a right target is important, finding a right advisor is as important for a successful M&A.

Comparisons of M&As and Other Forms of Alliances

Other forms of alliances can be understood better by comparing the pros and cons of each with those of M&As. Because alliances and M&As are often used to enter new business or markets (e.g., foreign markets), four options in the context of new business/market entry are compared.

Overall, there are four different options for entering a new business/market. A company can close a particular contract and ally with others. Franchising, one type of contractual alliance, is often seen in the fast food restaurant industry. Another way of allying with other companies is creating a joint-venture. A joint-venture is a new entity created and owned by two or more parent companies. As discussed, a company can acquire another company that already operates in the business/market. Of course, a company can enter by itself known as organic expansion. The general differences of these four forms of entry into a new business/market can be summarized as follows. Note that the speed and size of risk will depend on the size of investment. Accordingly, Table 6.2 suggests a general comparison of the four types of modes when expecting the similar size of operation (i.e., sales)

Contractual Alliance

In a broader sense, almost any business deal buying something from a supplier involves a contract. However, it is called a contractual "alliance" when the contract is long term and expects

Table 6.2 Comparison of four different entry modes

	Contractual alliance	Joint-venture	M&A	By itself
Speed	High	Medium	Low ~ Medium	Low
Return	Low	Medium	High	High
Risk	Low	Medium	High	High
Control	Low	Medium	Medium ~ High	High

cooperation with the two or more companies involved. It is well known that US car manufacturers used to focus too much on price and selected suppliers that offered the lowest price every year, making suppliers avoid long-term investments and lose competitiveness while Japanese car manufacturers cooperated with suppliers and developed "win–win" long-term relationships.[6]

A contractual alliance is relatively easy to form because the contents of an alliance are specific. Using the partners' strengths to complement the focal company's strengths is strategically a very useful idea. Of course, to successfully do so involves finding the right partner that has the complementary resources.

This mode is popular when a company wants to enter a foreign market. Because a company might have very limited knowledge of a foreign market, a company would want to find a partner that has the knowledge of the local market and can be responsible for marketing and selling, while the focal company is in charge of developing and manufacturing products, for example. Another example may be fast food chains such as McDonald's that had exclusive contracts with Disney to use characters from Disney to promote Happy Meals.

With a contractual alliance, however, a company only maintains a very weak form of control. Although contracts can determine the contents of the alliance, contracts cannot exhaust every possibility of the abuse or opportunistic behaviors of the partner.

Even when companies become large and more knowledgeable, the issue of control still remains. The experience of visiting McDonald's in different locations is a good example. While some are very good, others are average at best. Franchise contracts used by McDonald's have many rules, but the degree to which the rules are strictly followed depends on franchisees.

Joint-Venture

A joint-venture is similar to a contractual alliance in the sense that two or more companies bring their strengths and try to help each other and thus finding a right partner is very important. A joint-venture is different from contractual alliance in a way that all parents are responsible for the performance of the joint-venture, not a particular function. Think about the example of Sony-Ericsson, a cell phone manufacturing joint-venture created by Sony and Ericsson in 2001. Sony's marketing prowess combined with Ericsson's manufacturing experience with cell phones should make the joint-venture powerful enough to compete with rivals such as Nokia, Samsung, and Apple. Both Sony and Ericsson own a 50% share in the joint-venture. Because they own a 50% share, they have limited incentive to mess up the joint-venture for the sake of their own interest.

Meanwhile, a joint-venture is an option in which partners learn from each other.[7] To the extent that the joint-venture is created to compensate for the weakness of each other, each partner can exit from a joint-venture either when the weakness is learned or other partners' strengths are no longer attractive. Although cooperation is the key for the success of a joint-venture, competition to learn from the partner simultaneously takes place.

Even a joint-venture is not immune to abuse by one of the partners, particularly in unknown markets. Danone, a French food giant famous for its yogurt, learned a lesson the hard way when they exited joint-venture contracts with Shanghai entrepreneur Zong Qinghou. In 1996 Danone and Mr. Zong began developing joint-ventures under the name Wahaha, which Mr. Zong founded in the 1980s. While Danone owned 51% of about

40 joint-ventures, it was Mr. Zong that was in charge of operations in China. As a result of the joint-venture, the Wahaha
brand became one of the most famous in China. However,
according to Danone, Mr. Zong produced and sold Wahaha-
branded drinks independent of the joint-ventures using his own
networks. The dispute was eventually settled in 2009 as Danone
sold its 51% share.[8] Mr. Zong was later reported the richest Chinese with an estimated wealth of $12 billion in 2010.

M&As

As discussed, M&As are often used to buy resources, scale, and
time. It is important to note that the commitment and the size
of investment in an M&A is much larger than those in contractual alliances or JVs. To reach an agreement, an acquirer and a
target are often involved in an intensive negotiation. The assessment of the target company and resulting price is particularly
difficult to identify when the acquirer first enters a new business
or market. The negotiation becomes more complicated and
can be longer when there are multiple bidders attempting to
acquire the target. In this sense, it is possible that the speed is
not as high as contractual alliances or JVs. Research suggests
that companies often start with a contractual alliance and/or
joint-venture that are less costly and easy to form (and dis-
solve).[9] After obtaining some knowledge, it is much easier for
the acquirer to assess the value and purchase the target company with confidence.

By Itself

Finally, a company can enter a new business/market without
allying with others. By entering by itself, a company does not
have to worry about the opportunistic behavior of others or
about excessive investment for an acquisition. However, building a business from scratch takes time. Even if a company
recruits experienced personnel from other companies, it is difficult to form an organization where each person defines each
role clearly and collaborates with each other to reach the goal

of the organization. Meanwhile, by starting small, a company may be able to obtain important knowledge without a large investment relatively quickly. Starting small can also be a good way to collect information regarding potential alliance partners and acquisition targets.

Issues in Alliances and M&As

As a summary of this section, three important points need to be reiterated. First, as examined, each option of entry has pros and cons. A company needs to carefully consider each of the options before selecting a final one. Second, alliances or M&As cannot be done without interacting with other companies. Thus, it is important for a company to find a right partner or target. Even when a joint-venture appears to be the best option, a company might not be able to find a partner that agrees with the end goals. Moreover, a company has to offer something that is attractive to a partner so that a partner agrees to create a partnership. In this sense, a self-centered perspective needs to be corrected and a win–win partnership needs to be developed. Finally, alliances and M&As are never static. A company may select a contractual alliance today, but, in the future, the company may want to acquire the partner or even operate by itself. As a joint-venture is often characterized as a method for conducting a learning war, a company needs to have a dynamic view toward alliances and M&As.

International Strategy

Today, the question is not *whether* a company should go international. Instead, the question is *how* a company should go international. Given the availability of various communication tools and the quick proliferation of news at a worldwide level, the global market has become much closer than before. Moreover, it is clear that markets in developed countries are mostly matured. For further growth, developing countries that are located in Asia, Africa, and South America are important markets with great potential for companies to enter. In fact, although researches often divide M&As into domestic and international, most large M&As inevitably involve the integration of international operations as well.

Because the idea of pros and cons of entry mode in terms of contractual alliance, joint-venture, M&A, and by itself can be applicable to entry to international markets, this section focuses on two points particularly relevant in the context of the internationalization of a company: (1) standardization vs. local adaptation and (2) the psychic distance paradox

Dilemma of Internationalization

The first point is the inherent dilemma a company faces when entering an international market: Should it maintain the business model developed in the home country and pursue knowledge utilization and economies of scale or should it customize its business model to accommodate the needs and uniqueness of the host country? The former is often called a global strategy and the latter is referred to as a multi-domestic strategy. A global strategy is very popular among industrial products such as chemicals and products in the oil industry where the needs and specification of products across countries are relatively similar. In such cases, scale is the most important part of the strategy. As a result, most of the companies in chemical and oil industries are large, global players. A multi-domestic strategy can be seen in industries that need to take local differences into consideration. Retail and food businesses are a typical example. For example, McDonald's sells alcohol in Europe and shrimp burgers in Japan, neither of these items are sold in US operations.

Figure 6.1 **A framework for thinking international strategy.**

In many cases, companies need to have both responsiveness to local needs and consistency at global scale. Unless a company accommodates products to meet the needs (and regulations) of local markets, it is difficult to sell products. Just because a company is successful in the US or in Japan, it does not necessarily mean that the company following a similar strategy will be successful in China. However, if a company completely localizes its products and operation, it essentially becomes one of the local companies. To differentiate itself from local companies and maintain a competitive advantage, it has to use its global presence and scale. In this sense, a strategy that balances both localization and standardization is referred to a transnational strategy, while the difference between a true transnational strategy and stuck-in-the middle is not very large. Localization often sacrifices economies of scale, while standardization similarly leads to inadequate accommodation of local needs. Meanwhile, half-baked localization with mediocre standardization is unlikely to attract any customers. To pursue a transnational strategy, managers need to strike a fine balance between localization and standardization.

In the past, various companies tried to sell "world-model" products assuming that the global markets are becoming more and more common. By developing and selling a standardized product, companies can enjoy tremendous economies of scale. However, such trials have not been very successful except for the areas of industrial products and IT products (e.g., iPod). For example, both GM and Ford faced challenges when they tried to sell a "world-car," but they failed to overcome the challenges every time. In China, Kentucky Fried Chicken (owned by YUM brands) sells noodles, while Starbucks sells coffee, not teas that are traditionally popular in China, so that they can influence or even educate customers.[10]

The internationalization dilemma is not limited to products/services. Managing local subsidiaries is an important issue as well. For example, should human resource systems and functions such as evaluation and reward mechanisms in a local subsidiary be the same as those used in the home country? If the system needs to be modified, how much should it be modified? Besides the language and customs barriers, companies should pay careful attention to differences between cultures and ways of thinking across different countries. Companies need to take the differences into consideration in deciding how much of an original system should be maintained and how much should be changed to suit the preferences of the local employees. Again, if businesses models or internal systems are localized too much, it is difficult for a company to use the know-how developed in the home country to differentiate itself.

The bottom line is the importance of understanding the strengths of the company and utilizing those strengths, even in an international context. If the strengths are not utilized, the uniqueness of a company is lost, likely leading to failure. Meanwhile, it is not always important for a company to stick to its strengths as are. By utilizing the information and findings obtained in various countries, a company can actually evolve its strengths. It is even possible for a company to take a multi-domestic strategy first, and develop a global level strength and move to a transnational strategy.

Psychic Distance Paradox

The other important issue in relation to internationalization is the psychic distance paradox, which was proposed by two Canadian researchers, O'Grady and Lane, in 1996.[11] Their idea came from the observation that many successful Canadian retailers were unable to replicate their success in the US, which is a neighboring country. Essentially, the paradox is as follows: The closer two countries are, the smaller the cultural differences and differences in customer needs are, which should increase the likelihood of successes. However, the closer two countries are, the less sensitive to the differences between the two countries top managers become, which results in more failures. This taken-for-granted mind-set makes top managers blind to the important but small differences.

Interestingly, the opposite is also true. Many people argue that internationalization is not easy because of the many differences across countries. They can stress for example, how different the Chinese market or the Japanese market is from the US market. In fact, an American MBA student who came to Japan as an intern for Sony was surprised to be asked "Do you have a gun?" so many times.[12] To the extent that many US people still believe that there are many Samurais in Japan now (which is not correct), many Japanese people believe that all US people carry a gun or rifle. Such misleading illusions are partly attributable not only to movies and novels, but also to management books. Many management books stress the differences and scare readers. However, companies deal with people, who are fundamentally the same even if they live in the US, Japan, China, or Zimbabwe. They love family. They like to eat good food. And they feel unsatisfied, unhappy, or mad when they are treated unfairly.

In the face of a new market, managers should understand what is common and what is different. A new entry fails when managers ignore the differences between markets, however, it also fails just as often when managers pay little attention to the commonalities. In many cases, the fundamental strategy that succeeded in the home country still applies when the strategy is modified in response to the local needs of the host country appropriately.

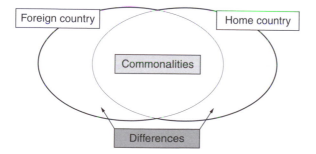

Figure 6.2 **An overarching framework for international expansion.**

CORE CASE: DAIMLER-CHRYSLER

In 1998, Daimler announced "a merger of equals" with Chrysler. The merger was welcomed with excitement. It was because the potential synergy between technology advancements and the strong presence in high-end markets of Daimler with the cost-competitiveness and strong presence in middle to lower and truck markets of Chrysler was estimated to be significant. As a result, the mass media repeatedly featured such discussions as "Only the top 5 automobile companies in the world will survive," "What Honda and BMW should do?" According to an article of the *Wall Street Journal* (May 8, 1998):

- The total synergy is estimated to be around $3 billion, which is more than 40% of the total profits of the two companies.
- One-third of the synergy is to come from efficiency in purchasing and logistics, one-third is to come from increasing sales due to common promotion and the efficient use of dealers, and one-third is to come from sharing R&D and technology.
- One analyst argued that the synergy could be $3 billion or even $5 billion per year.

However, two-and-a-half years later, the *Wall Street Journal* (October 27, 2000) reported:

- The expected $3 billion synergy was rarely realized.
- Daimler stopped calculating such synergy effects.

The failure of the merger (later, it became clearer that it was never "a merger of equals," but an acquisition of Chrysler by Daimler) provides important lessons, particularly given that Jergen Schremp, CEO of Daimler at the time of the merger, clearly stated that they understood the risks of such a large-scale merger and were prepared.

After the continued poor performance of Chrysler, the top management of Chrysler was fired and new management was sent from Daimler. While the turnaround seemed to be successful, Chrysler again went under water in 2005. Eventually, Chrysler was divested to a hedge fund, Cerberus in 2007.

Sources: Lipin, S. 1998. "Daimler-Chrysler merger to produce $3 billion in savings, revenue gains" *Wall Street Journal*, May 8; Ball, J., and Miller, S. 2000. "For two car giants, a megamerger isn't the road to riches" *Wall Street Journal*, October 27; Taylor III, A. 2008. "Can Chrysler survive?" *Fortune*, April 18.

Besides how misleading some of the Wall Street analysts were, the whole story provides important lessons to consider for M&As, particularly cross-border ones.

In finding a target for an M&A, it is common to consider a company that has complementary strengths and resources to develop a synergy (i.e., private synergy). That is one reason why an M&A is often equated with marriage. In this case, Daimler with advanced technology and a strong presence in the high-end auto market and Chrysler with its low-cost manufacturing capabilities and a strong presence in the middle- to lower-end auto market and the truck market seemed to be a great couple in the auto industry. They had limited overlap in product lines thus integration should have been smooth.

However, one important issue is often ignored in thinking about complementarities and synergy. The *synonym of complementary is different*. Looking for a company that has complementary resources and strengths means looking for a company that is very different from oneself. Daimler with its advanced technology targeting a high-end market developed people and culture that emphasized high quality over low cost. While Chrysler targeted middle- and low-end automobile customers it needed to consider low cost over high quality. Employees from each of the two different cultures found it difficult to agree on how to develop, manufacture, or promote a new car. In fact, it was not until 2001, three years after the merger, that Daimler and Chrysler started to discuss the idea of sharing common parts and it took another two years to actually implement it. Because they were different and complemented each other, it seemed as though it was worth being together. However, because they were so different, it was difficult to work together. This is an inherent dilemma of M&As.

Similar problems arise when students form study groups. To help each other and maximize the synergy across the group members, students want to work with people with different backgrounds and/or majors. However, because backgrounds and majors are so different, it is often difficult to agree and work together smoothly.

7

LEADERSHIP AND DECISION MAKING

Leadership

There are many books about leadership. Just a quick search on Amazon.com provides more than 10,000 books. Moreover, new books about leadership are published every year. Why are so many leadership books needed?

Leaders play an important role in organizations. Whether it is a for-profit company, a sports team, the military, or a country, a leader determines the performance of the organization and resulting welfare of the members. Accordingly, researchers have been working on understanding the profiles of good leaders. For example, the Big Five model, which uses five different dimensions to characterize a person's profile, has been used. The Big Five factors are Openness, Conscientiousness, Extraversion, Agreeableness, and Neuroticism or Need for emotional stability (OCEAN, or CANOE if rearranged). According to researches, a good leader can be characterized as visionary (O+); dedicated to a goal (C+); energetic, outgoing, and persuasive (E+); competitive (A–); and resilient (N–).[1] At a first glance this description appears to make a lot of sense. Meanwhile we also know that there have been and are successful leaders that do not necessarily fit the profile or have what would be considered unsuccessful leader traits. Likewise many examples are available of people who are not able to lead or be a leader that have all the characteristics. Some good leaders are more micro-oriented than visionary (e.g., Michael Eisner, former CEO of Disney, Mickey Drexler, former CEO of GAP and current CEO of JCREW). Other leaders are probably too visionary and committed to throwing good money after bad until it is too late. Moreover, a leader who was successful in one organization is not guaranteed to be successful in the other organizations (e.g., Paul Pressler who left Disney for GAP).

There is no silver bullet or equation that defines how to be a great leader. Reading many leadership books cannot make us good leaders. In fact, this is the same as good strategy. Reading many strategy books does not give us a good strategy. It is because strategy should be unique, based on the strengths of the company and external environment (customers, competition). Unless we clearly understand our strengths, how can we be a good leader? To be a good leader is not accepting or imitating stereotypes provided by books. Instead, being a good leader needs understanding oneself deeply in terms of strengths and weaknesses, identifying an organization that can best use your strengths, and finding partners that can complement your strengths. One can learn from others and from books, but it is important to develop a unique leadership style based on personal strengths.

Decision Making

Rational Decision Making

Decision making is one of the most important tasks of a leader. Besides many big decisions such as M&As and entry into foreign markets, a leader also needs to make decisions on almost every aspect of an organization including whom should be hired, how to allocate resources to different businesses, and when to stop or divest a poor performing business. Leaders (as well as us in general) strive for making the best decision for each business issue. Accordingly, there are many books, guidelines, and tactics that discuss "how to make a good decision."

Among others, Professors Hammond, Keeney, and Raiffa provide one model that can be used as a guideline to making rational decisions.[2] They call the model PrOACT, composed of

Problem
Objective
Alternatives
Consequences
Tradeoffs

By setting the right problem, making a clear objective, exploring alternatives, evaluating consequences and trade-offs, a decision maker should be able to find a good choice, if not the best possible choice. Additionally, they point out the influence of uncertainty, risk tolerance, and linked decisions on the focal decision.

It is particularly important to find the right problem. Decision makers often assume that the right problem is identified and thus focus much energy and time on finding and evaluating alternatives. However, as was discussed in relation to McDonald's mistake of targeting adult customers, good alternatives will never be found if a wrong problem is identified.

The baseline idea behind most decision making models is to be as rational as possible by considering all the information available. In other words, it is critical to collect information and analyze it to reach a good decision.

Biases in Decision Making

While it is clear that rationality is very important for making good decisions, it is also known that human beings are not always rational. In fact, humans are often biased and predictably irrational![3] Researchers have been examining various biases in relation to decision making.[4] The following are some major biases which are often apparent in managerial decision making:

1   Selectiveness. We tend to believe that we make decisions based on "facts." "Facts" are supposed to be objective and common regardless of who sees it. However, "facts" are not necessarily perceived equally by all the people.

The same facts can be seen differently depending on who is reading and interpreting them: more specifically, which view you have, what preconceived hypotheses one has, and what background knowledge one has. A classic example was shown by Hastrof and Cantril more than a half century ago.[5] After a very rough football game between Princeton and Dartmouth, students of each school reported how many fouls players of each team committed.

This phenomenon is more likely a daily experience than an exception. When a person attends a football or soccer game, they tend to think the referee is strict in judging the fouls on their team and generous or lenient toward the opponent. Interestingly, the audience of the other side feels exactly the opposite.

When managers want to initiate a new project or business, the same thing can happen. When they lead the project, they tend to think it is almost there. With a little more investment, the business will realize its potential. Meanwhile, people who opposed the project see exactly the same data and argue that the business is a waste of time and resources. The key here is not who is right or wrong. Instead, supposedly objective facts can be seen in very different ways. An old proverb says, "seeing is believing," but in reality, "we see what we believe."[6]

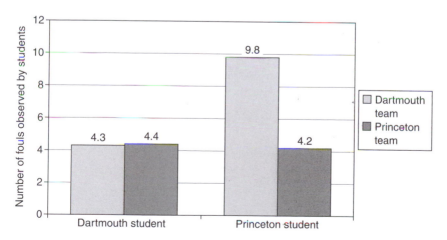

Figure 7.1 **Differences of fouls by observers.**

Another name for this tendency is prejudice. Prejudice is self-serving because people unconsciously pay attention to information that supports their prejudice. In many cases, you may not recognize when you are biased. When you recruit people, you have to be careful. When your candidate has a great track record or belonged to a good company such as GE or McKinsey, you tend to believe the candidate is good, even if the record was just luck. It is notable that Jack Welch, a former CEO of GE, points out that gut feeling is an important component of business decisions but that one should not rely on gut feeling in recruiting people because we can easily fall in love with a candidate.[7]

Harold Geneen, a legendary manager in the 1970s, critically stresses this point in his book, *Managing* (page 97):

There is no word in English language that more strongly conveys the intent of incontrovertibility, i.e., "final and reliable reality," than the word "fact." However, no word is more honored by its breach in actual usage.

For example, there are and we saw yesterday:

"Apparent facts."
"Assumed facts."
"Reported facts."
"Hoped-for facts."
"Facts" so labeled and accepted as facts – i.e., "accepted facts" and many similar derivations!

The highest art of professional management requires the literal ability to "smell" a "real fact" from all others – and moreover to have the temerity, intellectual curiosity, guts and/or plain impoliteness, if necessary, to be sure that what you do have is indeed what we will call an "unshakable fact."[8]

2 Recency bias. "Facts" can be particularly shaky when they are stored in memory and recalled. In this case, we tend to recall only things that are easily recallable. The more recent and the more vivid, the easier it is for us to recall, which is called recency biases. A particular project can be examined extensively when a similar project failed just recently. Similarly, a risky project may not when the failure was a long time ago and not many people feel the vividness of the failure any more.

In fact, memory is not as trustful as we think. A classic story can be seen in the recording of a psychology conference. After two weeks, participants forgot about 90% of what they discussed and the remaining 10% included a lot of mistakes.[9] Additionally, it has also been found that when eyewitnesses are asked to pick a suspect from a lineup, where all suspects stand shoulder-to-shoulder, eyewitnesses consistently make errors. Even when the real suspect is not in the lineup, witnesses often falsely finger the person who looks most like the suspect.[10]

In relation, Stephen Covey, famous for his bestseller, *The Seven Habits of Highly Effective People*,[11] points out the risks of recency and vividness in comparison with importance. When we use urgency and importance to form a matrix and plot our tasks we can see how we feel. Obviously, important and urgent tasks are priority number one and less important and less urgent tasks take lowest priority. The problem is determining number two and three. Although we all know that there are things that are not urgent but important thus we have to start working on them as soon as possible, such tasks are often postponed. Instead, we are overloaded with urgent tasks that seem to need immediate attention. We take care of urgent issues, usually without solving a fundamental problem. As a result, urgent but minor problems continue to emerge and consume our time, which should have been spent on important issues. As a result, this vicious cycle just keeps going.

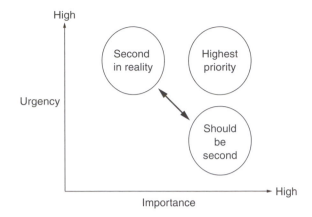

Figure 7.2 **Importance vs. urgency.**

3   Hindsight bias. In relation to the biases associated with memory, hindsight bias is another important and popular bias. In many cases, a decision is made under uncertainty. While it is easy to have all the information and all the alternatives clearly compared and objectively ranked, such cases are rare. Using an example of acquisitions, it is impossible to perfectly assess the amount of synergy beforehand. Yet, a manager needs to make a decision within a certain time period, which adds pressure. If a manager is unable to make a decision now, the target company may be acquired by a rival. Such opportunities may never arise again in the future. Thus, a manager must decide with limited information under the allotted time constraints. However, if the acquisition turns out to be a failure, managers and people involved are surprised to see many people argue such things as "I knew that." After the results are found, people tend to reconstruct their memories and behave as if they knew the results beforehand. However, more than likely, they did not know beforehand, but believe that they did. This bias has also been referred to as, the Monday football syndrome, as football fans comment on the results of the games on Sunday as if they could have done better than Tom Brady or Brett Favre.

Hindsight bias does not directly influence a particular decision. However, when managers do not pay attention to this bias, their capability to learn from failures will be significantly compromised. Managers will simply accuse those who are in charge as if they could have done better. If not accounted for, managers will ignore the difficulties of making a decision under uncertainty and miss opportunities to learn from mistakes and possibly adapt for future decisions.

Accordingly, it is important to be careful with case studies of successful or failed companies. Many analysts and writers create a story that fits the success or failure. Even if a particular company succeeded or failed by luck, such analysis tends to reconstruct the facts and logically explains the success or failure. When we examine only successful companies and try to find success factors by identifying factors common across those successful companies, it is possible to miss something important. However, it is possible that there were companies that had the features and still failed. Think about Cisco systems, a very successful high tech company. One major driver of its success is its series of acquisitions of small companies. If Cisco is analyzed and acquisitions are the key for success, the analysis is obviously missing the fact that there are many unsuccessful companies that acquired other companies.

4   Overconfidence. Confidence is often argued to be one of the most important characteristics of a leader. When a

	Successful companies	Unsuccessful companies
Factor A		?
Factor B	?	

Figure 7.3 **Importance to examine both successful and unsuccessful companies.**

leader does not look confident, employees are unlikely to commit themselves to a particular decision, even if the decision is a good one. Meanwhile, when a leader looks confident and determined, even a very difficult project can be accomplished by committed employees. As a result, self-confidence or self-efficacy is one of the most important goals for education.[12]

However, excessive confidence is not beneficial. In fact, people are often overconfident. Most students think that they are above average and more than half of the students think they are in the top 20%. Another research found that 94% of professors in a university believe that they are better than the average professor.[13] As a result, many accidents and failures result from overconfidence and underestimation of risks. It is well known that the minister of Ukraine publicly announced that the chance of accidents in their nuclear power plant was 1:10,000 years, just two months before the Chernobyl accident. NASA also stated that the probability of such large accidents as the Challenger explosion is a 1:100,000 chance.[14] Other research suggests that people tend to be more overconfident in answering questions that are moderately or extremely difficult and less overconfident in answering familiar questions.[15] Jergen Schremp, from Daimler-Chrysler, also publicly announced that they examined and understood the risks of a large merger and they would be able "to beat the statistics – 70% of mergers have not brought results."[16]

It is interesting that the degree of confidence and the degree of correctness are not related. It has also been found that an increase of information increases the confidence, but not the correctness. To the extent that information is assessed selectively with current perspectives, this result is not surprising. UC Berkley Professor Tetlock points out that experts' forecasts are not as good as simple extensions of the past data.[17] According to him, the difference between experts and lay people are not the degree of correctness but the degree of confidence and the number of reasons (and excuses).

It is certainly important to show your confidence to others. At the same time, you have to ask yourself whether you are overconfident and missing something important. In general, pessimistic leaders are not very popular. However, given that success contributes to overconfidence through mass media,[18] often unconsciously, maintaining healthy pessimism is important for avoiding mistakes from overconfidence.

5 Anchoring. When people are provided a certain starting point, they tend to use the point in estimating the value of something, even if the point is groundless or irrelevant. Such tendency is called anchoring. Researchers have found that people are even influenced by a random number used as an anchor generated by rootlet.

Anchoring is quite popular in everyday life. When people visit a local grocery store, BestBuy, or Amazon. com they find a price tag that is crossed out by a red dash with a new price on it, saying 30% or 40% off. Consumers typically do not know how the initial price is set, but feel that they are receiving a better deal when the price is reduced by 30% in comparison with an initial price (anchor). It is also well known that real estate agents tend to show a poor or excessively expensive house to clients first (anchor) and show a house they want to sell later. In comparison with the first one, clients find the second one much more attractive.

In the context of decision making in business, past performance and performance of the competitors often play the role of an anchor. Even if the external environment completely changes or if budgeting is drastically different from year to year. Similarly, executives often feel better when main competitors perform poorly, even if their own company performs poorly. Although it is important to compete with rivals, being overly concerned with comparisons may be harmful, particularly when the underlying strategy is different. Such concerns can mislead top managers to imitate a competitor and undermine the distinctiveness of its own strategy or strengths. One such example could be seen in Merrill Lynch. Stan O'Neal, the former CEO of Merrill Lynch, was famous for constant comparison of his company with Goldman Sachs. Every time Goldman's performance was better than that of Merrill, he was so demanding to subordinates to the point that "you didn't want to be in the office on Goldman earnings day," a comment reported in the *Wall Street Journal.* His quest to compete with and outperform Goldman changed the culture of Merrill and led the company to riskier areas such as underwriting collateralized debt obligations, resulting in further deterioration of its performance.[19] He was eventually fired in October, 2007.

In this sense, it is important to set appropriate goals for new projects. A new business involves a large amount of uncertainty and thus setting a goal is often arbitrary. Yet, the arbitrary goal often influences the subsequent decisions and actions. Accordingly, managers must understand the anchoring effects and the need to be flexible as new information is obtained. Labeling successes and/or failures by whether performance exceeds initial expectations can potentially mask important aspects, as success or failure is mostly determined by the initial goal, as opposed to the strategy and execution of the strategy.

In relation to anchoring, status quo (or default mode) often has a strong influence on individuals and organizations. In general, people are more comfortable sticking to the status quo than changing it. An interesting example is the difference in registration rates for organ donation across countries measured in 2003. Although France and Austria have a 99% rate, the US only has a 28% rate, and England has a 17% rate, while Germany which shares a similar culture and language with Austria only has a 12% rate. The difference simply comes from opt in or opt out. In countries where people need to opt out, the registration remains very high, while other countries that require opt in for registration have limited percentage of population registered. The status quo matters.[20]

Good Biases and Bad Biases

It is important to think why we have these biases. In fact, most of the biases are good in terms of saving on the load of required information processing. As discussed in the beginning of this section, people tend to have a perspective and/or a hypothesis. Without these, people would have to evaluate every piece of information from every angle. By developing a certain way of processing information, such burdens can be avoided. Similarly, recency bias and anchoring are helpful in allowing managers to focus attention on something generally important. Confidence is important to execute something and hindsight bias is a result of our tendency to understand particular events from the perspective of means and ends associations. In other words, these biases are not inherently bad. Most of the time, the biases are helpful but when excessively or inappropriately used, such biases are harmful.

Given that biases are often unconscious, it is practically impossible "to be careful" by ourselves. Instead, it is more practical to have a good advisor, mentor, or partner who can point out the biases from an outside perspective. In this sense, it is probably not a coincidence that many successful start-up companies are founded by two people. Hewlett-Packard, Sony, Microsoft, Apple, and Honda are a few notable examples. Although the value of partnering is often narrowly discussed from the perspective of functional complementarities, the importance of having someone whom you can trust and who can give honest opinions should not be underestimated.

Decision Change

While it is obviously important to make a good decision, current changing and uncertain environments make mistakes by managers almost inevitable. Although "wait and see" is one alternative in such rapidly changing environments, it is impossible to objectively know when the right time to move is. Regardless of what type of decision is made, there is always a possibility for making mistakes. In this sense, changing a decision at an appropriate time is as important as making a good decision.

Escalation of Commitment

To the extent that a new strategy or initiative involves unexpected problems and challenges, a new strategy or project will never be successful without a commitment to overcome such obstacles. For example, Corning took more than ten years and $100 million – overcoming high market skepticism and middle management resistance – to launch its optical fibers business.[21] Konosuke Matsushita, the founder of Panasonic, stated that the primary determinant of success is to remain committed until success is achieved. Meanwhile, excessive commitment to a "wrong strategy" only exacerbates the bad situation. Such cases of throwing good money after bad are called escalation of commitment.

Researchers have pointed out various types of factors that cause escalation of commitment. Such factors include the amount of investment (project related factors), optimism, self-justification, emotional commitment, sunk-cost biases (decision-maker related factors), rules, politics (organizational factors), and expectation of success (social factors).[22]

Although we can identify factors that contribute to escalation, it still remains difficult for managers to exit. This is partly because the final results are never truly known. Theoretically, it is impossible to deny the possibility that an unsuccessful project may become successful if the project is committed to for one more month. In fact, it generally takes a few years for a new product to get popular. It took the VCR six years to take off or to achieve an average sales gain of about 40%.[23] The decision to stop or continue is one of the most important and challenging decisions top managers face.[24]

Strategic Flexibility

To avoid escalating commitment while managing projects in uncertain environments, a company requires strategic flexibility. Strategic flexibility can be defined as a company's capability to identify major changes in the external environment (e.g., introduction of disruptive technologies), to quickly commit resources to new courses of action in response to the change, and to recognize and act promptly when it is time to halt or reverse such resource commitments.[25]

To obtain strategic flexibility, there are three important components. First, without paying attention to the outcomes of strategic initiatives, it is impossible to consider whether an initiative should be stopped or if the initiative should be continued. Second, once attention is paid, objective assessment of the initiative is required. Third, after an assessment is made, a company needs to quickly act to further commit or reverse the course. While the importance of attention, assessment, and action seems to be obvious, there are a number of barriers in relation to various biases discussed in the previous section. Such barriers and conditions that can increase the barriers are summarized in Table 7.1.

An inability to attend, assess, and act can lead to a vicious cycle. When attention is limited, negative information from or regarding the project is unlikely to be caught. As a result, assessment becomes overly optimistic, resulting in less urgency to initiate an act. When nothing changes, the same pattern of attention continues and only positive information is captured. Such a cycle continues until things become very bad and by this time it is often too late.

It is difficult to avoid such vicious cycles and obtain strategic flexibility. Although there is no panacea or secret formula,

Table 7.1 Barriers to strategic flexibility

Component	Barriers	Conditions that increase barriers

Attention	• Complacent mind-set/decision rules (including hubris)
	• Organizational inertia
	  – Institutionalizing initial decisions by rules and routines
	  – Ignoring ideas and actions that deviate from the routines
		• Past success experience
		• Long tenure of top management
		• High age and size of an organization

Assessment	• Self-justification • Framing effects (managers tend to take risks in the face of losses) • Organizational politics	• Large size project (that result in large commitment and loss) • Weak governance • Organizational and social culture that are harsh on mistakes
Action	• Perceived uncertainty to the prospect of the project • Resistance to change	• High environmental uncertainty • Financial resource availability

Source: Adapted from Shimizu, K, and Hitt, M.A. 2004. Strategic flexibility: Organizational preparedness to reverse ineffective strategic decisions. *Academy of Management Executive*, 18 (4): 44–59.

there are three major issues. First, biases are unconscious. Top managers are prepared before they are overconfident or accustomed to the status quo. Once managers are overconfident, they will not know, because they evaluate themselves from the overconfident mind-set. Second, to minimize uncertainty, the results of initiatives need to be measured. Although some results are hard to measure, such difficulty should not be used as an excuse. Unless the outcomes are measured, it is almost impossible to assess initiatives, which will result in continuous commitment. Finally, top management should consider a portfolio of initiatives as opposed to a specific initiative. Given the limited resources, allocating such resources becomes critical. Although a particular initiative may seem to have some potential, others may have more and projects should be terminated if opportunities to invest in more promising ones arise. By using other projects as a reference point, assessment should be easier.

Decision making and decision change are both difficult. It is almost impossible to reach an optimum point. Probably that is why there are successful companies and unsuccessful companies. Top managers must continue efforts to make better decisions. Because decision making is difficult, a small additional effort can make a large difference over time.

CORE CASE: GAP

GAP started as a retailer of Levi's jeans in 1969. GAP struggled after man-ufacturers' price control broke down and competition intensified. When Mickey Drexler joined GAP in 1983, he initiated drastic changes including termination of all the private labels, focusing on basics such as Khakis and button-down shirts. He further shifted Banana Republic from Safari and opened a new brand, Old Navy, in 1994. From 1989 through 1998, the average return to investors was 38.8%, exceeding top companies such as Coca-Cola (35.3%), Nike (31.4%), and Disney (21.6%).

Despite his success, Drexler kept saying, "Think negative five comp." He was afraid of being complacent and tried to be as pessimistic as pos-sible. He had been a micro-manager who wanted to pay attention to every aspect of the company.

His mantra was "selling GAP as wide as Coca-Cola." Accordingly, he consistently stressed the importance of minimizing opportunity loss. He opened many stores every year, even after sales per store started declin-ing and insisted to stock every color and every size.

As the size of the company continued to grow, he gradually delegated some of the responsibilities. However, the delegation resulted in some of the brands' shift from basics to trendy fashion, losing core customers. GAP was full of conflicts and many veterans left for competitors around 2000. In 2002, Drexler was replaced by Paul Pressler who was known for the successful expansion of the Disney store and was one of the candid-ates for the next CEO of Disney.

Pressler was said to be the opposite of Drexler in every aspect. He was strong in numbers and made a drastic cost reduction, recovering GAP's performance quickly. However, when the issue shifted from cost cutting to increasing sales, his analytical approach backfired. He was not able to communicate with creative designers and often ended up with low-risk, non-unique products. Further, he did not resolve conflicts between store managers and designers. His focus was always on efficiency, leading to the departure of many creative people from GAP.

His only initiative was opening "Force & Stone" in 2005, targeting middle-aged women. Obviously, the brand was not consistent with what GAP did. In 2007, the brand closed as Pressler was fired.

Sources: Gap; Munk, N. 1998. "Gap gets it" *Fortune*, August 3, 68–82; Merrick, A. 2007. "Gap will fashion its future without Pressler" *Wall Street Journal*, January 23; Lee, L. 2007. "Paul Pressler's fall from the Gap" *Business Week*, February 26, 80–84; Covert, J., and Merrick, A. 2007. "Gap reverses Pressler, shuts a niche chain" *Wall Street Journal*, February 26.

In the 1980s and 1990s, Drexler led GAP strongly by showing consistency and flexibility. Based on his vision that GAP should become as popular as Coke, he expanded GAP by taking a risk of overstocking. He was also quick in terminating or changing unsuccessful brands. Besides getting rid of all the private labels, he rebranded Banana Republic (with a loss of $6.8 million). Even Hemisfie, a new brand he initiated, was killed two years after it was initiated once it was assessed as having no future. Such consistent actions provided a clear signal to employees in terms of what GAP was aiming for and how decisions needed to be made.

However, as the size of the company grew, his style no longer worked effectively. As a pessimistic and decisive leader, he made many changes. The repeated changes worked partly because the organization was not large and there were a number of lieutenants who supported Drexler and bridged the gap between Drexler and front-line employees. When the total number of stores exceeded 1000 and sales became more than $5 billion, every small change could cost the company a lot. Furthermore, communication between Drexler and others became more and more difficult.

Pressler replacing Drexler was an optimistic analyst. While Drexler was pessimistic and more of a micro-manager, Pressler was optimistic and caring. Compared to Drexler who acted based on his instincts and made decisions very quickly, Presler analyzed data carefully and made many rational choices, which initially contributed to the recovery of GAP significantly. However, compared to slashing costs, increasing sales involved more uncertainty and risks. To the extent Pressler relied on data in making a decision, he was slower and more vague in making decisions than Drexler and that influenced the future of GAP.[26]

The comparison of the two CEOs of GAP provides some important balances top managers need to pay attention to, even outside the fashion industry. First, continuity versus change. Drexler was initially very successful. However, as success continued and organizational size increased, his formula became outdated. Although one may stick to a familiar strategy, such strategies need to be refined as external environments and organizations change. Second, optimism versus pessimism. Employees like confident and optimistic leaders. However, such leaders can be more subject to complacency and escalation of commitment. To avoid such risks, one may want to be intentionally pessimistic, never be satisfied, and look for negatives, even though such pessimistic CEOs are unlikely to be popular. Third, individual intuition versus organizational consensus. Initially, almost all important decisions were made by Drexler. It worked partly because he was dedicated, knowledgeable, and sensitive in the company. However, as GAP became bigger, the workload grew tremendous. He needed to delegate some tasks. However, because he made all decisions himself, GAP did not develop experienced managers. As a result, the more Old Navy and GAP followed trendy fashion, the more they lost their distinctiveness and loyal customers. Pressler was more of a democratic leader. Unfortunately, his decisions did not seem to go beyond data.[27] This was partly because he did not have any advisors who were familiar with the fashion industry. In fact, his number two person in GAP was his subordinate at Disney. As a result, most of the decisions were based on consensus, which often result in Bs, no Cs, but no As either.

At the end of the day, leadership can be characterized as the management of dilemmas. Management is full of dilemmas, starting with managing sales and costs. The three dilemmas illustrated by GAP are particularly important ones. There is no silver bullet in terms of how to manage the dilemmas. Each leader needs to understand his or her strengths and weakness, find a partner who can provide not only complementary resources but also give candid opinions, and make decisions (Drexler and Pressler could have been a great team). It is good to be confident in front of employees, but being pessimistic also helps.

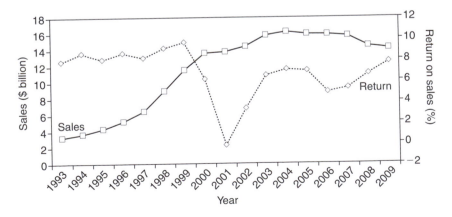

Figure 7.4 **Performance of GAP, 1993–2009.**

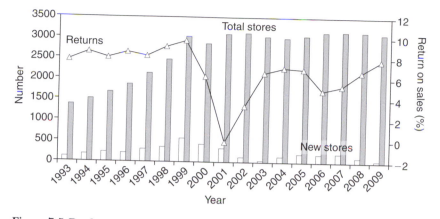

Figure 7.5 **Performance and number of stores of GAP** (source: GAP Annual Report).

8

STRATEGY
IMPLEMENTATION

In the face of changing customer needs, technology, and competition, organizations need to develop new strategies and adapt to new environments. Ironically, such rapid and frequent environmental changes that make it important to develop new strategies also make it difficult to formulate a "complete" strategy. Instead, a new strategy needs to be continuously refined in response to changing environments. Accordingly, performance is determined less by strategy per se than by the quality of its implementation. Jamie Dimon, CEO of J.P. Morgan Chase went so far as saying, "I'd rather have a fast-rate execution and second-rate strategy anytime than a brilliant idea and mediocre management."[1] More recently, in response to a 2008 survey by the Conference Board, 190 executives pointed out that the most important concern is "excellence of execution," followed by the "consistent execution of strategy by top management," and "speed, flexibility, and adaptability to change."[2]

Traditionally, strategy implementation receives less attention than strategy formation, particularly in the US. This is most likely due to the assumption that strategy formation is the task of top management and implementation only involves the actions following the instructions articulated by the formulated strategy. However, as pointed out by many executives, strategy implementation is no longer a peripheral that top management can ignore. Instead, as Larry Bossidy, the former executive of GE and Chairman of Honeywell points out, "Tactics are central to execution, but execution is not tactics. Execution is fundamental to strategy and has to shape it."[3] Yet, it is reported that more than 60% of employees of 1000 organizations across 50 countries (surveyed between 2003 through 2008) perceive that their organizations have low implementation capabilities.[4]

Barriers to Effective Strategy Implementation

In many cases, implementation failures are attributed to organizational structure and reward systems. Although it is certainly true that a strategy that is not supported by an organizational structure and is inconsistent with reward systems will not be successful, there are other important problems. Research suggests various reasons for implementation failures.[5] These reasons can be summarized into three causes: unexpected problems, unclear roles and responsibilities, and conflicts and misunderstandings within an organization. All these problems are exacerbated by environmental uncertainty.

Unexpected problems:

- unexpected moves by competitors
- unexpected responses by customers

Unclear roles and responsibilities:

- actions required to execute not clearly defined
- unclear responsibility

Conflicts and misunderstandings within an organization:

- lack of communication about the new strategy and environments
- conflicts among departments (ineffective coordination)
- information gap between top management and rank-and-file employees

---

The problem does not stop here, unfortunately. The key words derived from the research of implementation failure are "uncertainty" and "unclarity." As a result, many organizations try to solve implementation problems by articulating strategy with further analysis and data. However, such articulation will not easily solve the problems. To the extent that competitive and technological environments change quickly, the articulation of a strategy can result in a strategy becoming overly rigid. When the gap between a strategy and environments widens, the gap between top managers and rank-and-file employees also increases. While top managers may believe that a strategy is good, front-line employees may struggle with what is perceived as an outdated strategy. The roles and responsibility determined earlier are no longer effective, developing confusion and unclarity within an organization. Rather than solving the problem, articulation of strategy may only make things worse. When top management does not understand the problem, this vicious cycle continues and organizational performance continues to decline, despite the fact that everyone within an organization is working hard.

Social psychologist, Karl Weick also points out,

> *[Plans] also deceive us into thinking that we know more than we do. The worst aspect of plans is that they heighten the tendency to postpone action when something unexpected happens. People do nothing while they stand around asking themselves, "What was I supposed to do in this kind of emergency?"*[6]

Toward Effective Strategy Implementation: What is Communication?

As pointed out, the more top management tries to clarify and specify the details of a strategy, the more likely that such details

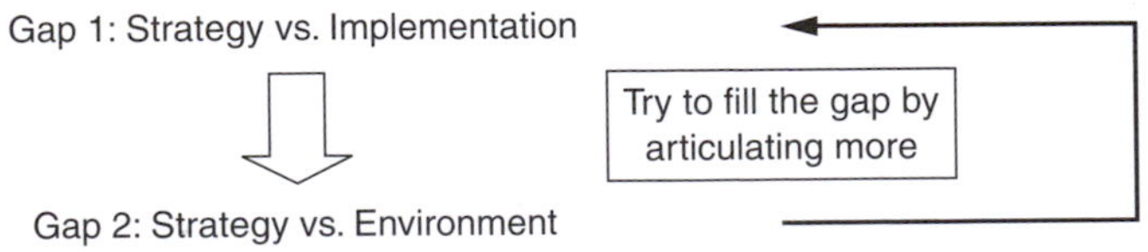

Gap 1: Strategy vs. Implementation

Try to fill the gap by articulating more

Gap 2: Strategy vs. Environment

Figure 8.1 **Vicious cycle of planning.**

will not fit with the new environment, which creates confusion at the front level. In this sense, strategy implementation should not be regarded as a linear process, i.e., strategy is first formulated by top management and then implemented by rank-and-file employees. Instead, strategy needs to be temporal and thought to be an iterative process of implementation and refinement.[7]

A temporal and inherently incomplete strategy has various holes and ambiguities. Implementation of such a strategy needs intensive communication within an organization to fill the holes and make sense of ambiguities. Communication plays a key role in successful strategy implementation as a tool for accumulating different findings and ideas across an organization, coordinating such different ideas, and sharing outcomes and their reasons within the organization.

An organization consists of departments (and people) with conflicting goals.[8] While the marketing department may want to spend more money, accounting departments like to minimize expenses. The R&D department wants more advanced technology and functions, while the manufacturing department pursues standardization and simplification, yet the sales department demands lower prices with higher value. To integrate these conflicting roles and pursue total optimization as an organization, coordination through communication is inevitable.

What is Not Communication?

Before discussing the importance of communication further, it may be a good idea to note what is *not* communication, at least communication that is necessary for strategy implementation. Communication is a widely used (or abused) word and scant attention is paid to it. From emails and twitter, phone, to face-to-face conversation, there are so many tools for communication. As long as a certain message is sent from a sender to a receiver, can it be called communication?

The answer is *no.* Although it is generally thought that communication is exchanging information, this is not enough when thinking about strategy implementation. Suppose that a new idea is found to attract customers and the idea is sent to a manager. The idea is sent because someone believes the idea is important, but why is the idea important? Unless the thought process is also understood by a boss or manager, the idea will never be understood correctly. In other words, communication is not just about sending information. *Communication is an interaction between a sender and a receiver to make the sender's objective understood by the receiver.*

Exchanging emails per se is rarely communication. Emails are a very efficient tool to send information, but not a good way to make objectives understood. It is because such tools cannot send contextual information. Think about a short sentence, "You are crazy." This sentence has various meanings and the meaning totally depends on the context. In fact, research reports that words contribute to only 7% of communication while facial expressions and body language contribute 55%, and tone of voice contributes to 38% of communication.[9] Unfortunately, such facts are forgotten and people tend to rely on emails and twitters these days. The side effects are significant. Research shows that the number of emails negatively contributes to the total amount of communication.[10] By using PCs and smart phones, we falsely believe that we become smart!

Face-to-face meetings are a powerful way of communicating. However, it is notable that such meetings have their own caveats. The idea that face-to-face meetings are a good way of communicating depends on two assumptions:

1 total amount of information of an individual < total amount of information of a group;
2 the amount of information of an individual increases through face-to-face meeting with group members.

However, such things do not always happen.[11] In many cases, the content of communication in meetings is already shared information. Even if an agreement seems to be reached, such agreement can simply be a reconfirmation of the information or agreement they had before the meeting. As a result, unique information individuals have may not be shared, which is often called "hidden profile." The problem of hidden profile is particularly salient when subordinates are communicating with their bosses. A meeting that confirms already known ideas is hardly communication.

What is Communication?

Earlier, communication was defined as an interaction between a sender and a receiver to make the sender's objective understood by the receiver. Many people use different modes of communication depending on the objectives. For sharing data and facts, email is a good tool. To share more complicated matters, face-to-face meetings are inevitable. What is often missing within an organization is the common understanding of why a particular mode is selected. Even if a mode is intentionally set such as a meeting to discuss a particular issue, rather than sending the information by email and asking inputs by email, colleagues and subordinates may not understand why the mode of communication (i.e., meeting) was selected. In such a case, people often argue that they have too many unproductive meetings and may even start to become late to attending the meetings. When members are not motivated to attend meetings, the outcome quality of the meeting will naturally be low. Such a self-fulfilling cycle can easily emerge in everyday life in an organization, particularly when efficiency and short-term performance are highly emphasized. Communication works only when both senders and receivers understand why a particular mode of communication is needed. Communication is an activity that works on the shared foundation among organization members, which needs communication.

Communication is a means, not a goal. Unfortunately, sometimes the notion that "we communicated" is believed to be more important than what was achieved through communication. This means and ends problem in communication is particularly popular in relation to performance evaluation. Here is a quote from Jack Welch's book, *Winning*:

> "How many of you have received an honest, straight-between-the-eyes feedback session in the last year, where you came out knowing exactly what you have to do to improve and where you stand in the organization?"
>
> On a good day, I get 20% of the hands up. Most of the time, it is closer to 10%.
>
> Interestingly, when I turn the question around and ask the audience how often they've given an honest, candid appraisal to their people, the numbers don't improve much.
>
> Forget outside competition when your own worst enemy is the day you communicate with one another internally![12]

The story of Jack Welch combined with the issue of a "hidden profile" gives us an important insight about the communication. *Communication is valuable when you do not like to communicate.* If you know that the receivers will agree cheerfully, many people have no problem with communication. But such an agreement may be because senders and receivers have the same idea before the actual communication takes place. Such comfortable communication achieves nothing new except for formality. In the meantime, when the response of the receivers is uncertain or possibly negative, communication becomes difficult. This happens when bosses stick to an initial idea that employees may think is no longer valid in a changing environment or when another department seems to pursue local optimization that damages the overall interest of the organization. This is exactly when communication is important. A boss or other departments may have invisible reasons for following the actions they are following. Through communication, senders and receivers will share different ideas and such interaction opens up a "win–win" solution or at least a mutual understanding. Again, communication is necessary especially when it is uncomfortable to do so.

As discussed in the section on synergy, value will be created when different possibly conflicting ideas complement each other and something new is developed. In this sense, communication within an organization is something tedious and time consuming. When communication is difficult, yet something must be communicated, there is a chance to create value. Communication is a critical activity within an organization in implementing strategy.

Communication and PDCA

In an uncertain and changing environment, strategy is often tentative and needs to be continuously improved through implementation. PDCA cycle, which comes from quality management and indicates Plan, Do, Check, and Action, is applicable to the iterative processes involved in implementation. In this process, communication contributes to the "plan" by accumulating and sharing data and ideas within an organization. Communication also contributes to the "do" or execution by coordinating different people and departments. Without communication, outcomes and their reasons (Check) cannot be shared within the organization. Through communicating such reasons and coordination of ideas for improving the initial strategy, the strategy is refined and further implemented (Action).

There are three important issues to effectively utilize communication in relation to PDCA.

First, to coordinate different ideas and findings, an organization has to have a foundation. Such a foundation can be called a vision, mission, or an organization's goal. Unless a core exists, collecting different ideas and findings ends up in amalgam, not integration. Only when there is a core, can the differences be integrated. As discussed in Chapter 1, a vision or mission cannot be stated and decorated with vague words. If top management is satisfied with the mission or vision that can be applicable to any company (i.e., we contribute to the welfare of the society), the organization is unlikely to effectively

implement a strategy. Yvon Chouinard, the founder of Patagonia once said, "If you're not pissing off 50% of the people,
you're not trying hard enough."[13]

Second, in finding and learning new ideas and information
in the process of implementation, organizational members
may encounter something new or something unexpected that
they are unfamiliar with. In such cases, it is often difficult to
explain these experiences. Rather than using conventional
words or concepts that are readily available, members need to
think, possibly about using analogies, to try and approach and
understand such new findings as closely as possible.[14] If members use conventional concepts and believe that they understand, they may miss something very important that is hidden
between the conventional concepts and the findings they
actually see.

For example, think about a strategy using an acquisition.
Researchers and consultants provide various reasons why
acquisitions often fail. Such reasons include over payment,
misunderstandings of potential synergy, and cultural clashes
(see Chapter 6). Although it is important to understand such
general risks, those major reasons rarely explain all the differences between success and failure among acquisitions. In fact,
most rigorous academic research only explains 30% or 40% of
the variances. In other words, at least 50% are factors unique
to the particular acquisition. If members are satisfied with a
conventional explanation, they miss the important 50% or
more from which important lessons can be learned.

Finally, utilizing PDCA cycles requires intensive communication across departments as well as across hierarchies. In
many cases, Plan and Check are done by upper managers and
rank-and-file managers and employees are in charge of Do
and Action. The communication is heavily skewed with quan-
titative information, i.e., numbers. However, as discussed,
numbers without contextual information are misleading. Is a
5% increase resulting simply from growth of the market
or from exceptional efforts of the front-line employees?

Moreover, summarized data may miss something important. For example, overall average numbers give us a good summary, but it masks the various kinds of different information behind the numbers. An average of 10% can be obtained with 1% and 19% as well as 10% and 10%. We all know that no family has 1.9 children.

To fill the gap between the top and the bottom of the hierarchy, it is important to include qualitative and contextual information in the communication across the hierarchy. Additionally, top managers can consider visiting the front-line and customers, so that they can obtain a perspective and feel the real life battle. Finally, in relation, the role of middle managers is also important. As "linking pins" between top management and lower level employees, middle managers can potentially make sense of up-to-date front level information from a strategic perspective, develop new and innovative ideas, and lead strategic change during implementation by involving both top management and rank-and-file employees.[15]

CORE CASE: HONDA

Honda first entered into the US market back in 1959. At that time, Honda was a motorcycle company and tried to sell its relatively large models, 250cc and 305cc. After its tremendous success, Honda's strategy was analyzed as a textbook case. According to the report from the Boston Consulting Group, Honda penetrated the US market with lower costs based on economies of scale and learning effects compared to domestic competitors and captured customers who were not traditional bikers.

However, when Professor Pascale at UCLA interviewed executives, the story was totally different. It is true that Honda tried to sell its big models, but the initial trial was a complete failure. Honda missed the bike season, which traditionally runs between April and August. The main models of the 250cc and the 305cc needed to be fixed dramatically because of oil leakage. Honda did not know how long and how hard the US people used bikes until they sold their bikes in the US. They mostly used precious cash to send those defects back to Japan by air.

As a result, they only had small bikes left. Because Honda people believed, "everything is big in the US," they never thought about selling their 50cc bikes in the US. Instead, they used such bikes for their own (such as for shopping). Somehow, a Sears buyer contacted them. Because they had nothing else, they made a deal. To their surprise, Sears started selling Honda's 50cc bikes in the sporting goods area and that is how many ordinary people started buying Honda bikes.

Sources: Pascale, R.T. 1984. "Perspectives on strategy: The real story behind Honda's success". *California Management Review*, 26 (3), 47–72; Pascale, R.T. 1996. "The Honda effect". *California Management Review*, 38 (4), 80–91.

CORE CASE: SUSHI ZUSHI

Sushi Zushi, a restaurant chain characterized by serving both traditional sushi and "innovative sushi," was founded by Alfonso Tomita on December 12, 2001. In ten years, it has successfully expanded and now operates seven restaurants in San Antonio, Dallas, and Austin, Texas.

Alfonso calls his last ten years an "entrepreneurial journey." He was initially planning to open a Mexican restaurant in San Antonio. However, strong opposition from his children changed his mind. After completing his strategic plan and ready to open the first restaurant in three months, he encountered 9/11. Although most people (including a counselor of an entrepreneur support center in a local university) opposed the idea of opening a new restaurant just three months after 9/11, two people supported him. One was a local fish supplier and the other was an owner of a restaurant. The owner suggested that a bad economy creates an opportunity to obtain good deals in terms of rent and hiring. With strong support from his family, he took a risk of opening Sushi Zushi as planned. In November, Alfonso was able to hire Luis Ramirez, a good sushi chef, who could not find a job in Dallas after the restaurant he was with just burned out.

According to his strategic plan, Sushi Zushi was supposed to "operate like a Subway, with the personality of Starbucks, and the food display and service concept of Corner Bakery or La Madeleine." By using franchising, Alfonso planned to open 1000 restaurants by 2010. When Luis first heard the idea, he immediately denied it. Luis argued that what customers wanted was not self-service, but nice food with a great atmosphere. Alfonso listened. The first restaurant generated positive cash flow from the first month.

By late 2009, Sushi Zushi hired experienced managers in restaurant operation, human resources, accounting, and construction. Alfonso was happy with the new set of managers. However, he found that Sushi Zushi had lost money in October 2010, which never happened before. He was shocked. He stated, "I was complacent after being able to hire many good people. They are good, but they do not know much about Sushi Zushi. I should have communicated more and led more."

After dramatically improving the performance in December 2010, Alfonso and his team strive to open 40 restaurants by 2020.

Source: interviews with Sushi Zushi.

Compared to 50 years ago when Honda entered into the US market, the concept of strategy is much more popular. We see many books about strategy and strategic management as well as many strategy consultants. In fact, Alfonso went to business school and learned how to develop a business plan for Sushi Zushi.

However, learning strategy does not guarantee the success of a company. First, strategy is mainly built on analyses of internal and external environments (3Cs). To the extent that managers of a company rationally analyze and develop a strategy, so do managers of competitors. In other words, if a company logically comes up with a particular move, competitors of the company also understand what move the company will initiate. To this end, differentiation may not be so easy. Second, external environments change very rapidly. Such changes as globalization, emerging markets, and technological development accelerate both the types and magnitude of changes in the environment. Even if a company analyzes the environment very rigorously, such analyses may not be useful when environments change. Finally, in relation, strategy is a plan for the future. As we all know, you cannot completely predict the future. Many unexpected things, both good things and bad things, can happen in life.

It does not mean that strategy and understanding strategy is useless. Quite the opposite is true. Because almost every company has a strategy, it is fatal for a company not to have a strategy! Honda's mistakes such as not researching customers or not building appropriate products are inexcusable now. However, good strategy does not automatically deliver good results. Strategy needs to be effectively implemented. Moreover, such implementation inherently accompanies learning and improvements, as environmental changes and unexpected events are inevitable, which both Honda and Sushi Zushi encountered in both good ways and bad ways.

One may call the success of Honda and Sushi Zushi as totally dependent on luck. Yes, we cannot deny the fact that they were lucky. Unless a Sears buyer found Honda's small bikes and sold them in the sporting goods area, Honda may not be as successful or at least it may have taken more time. For Sushi Zushi, 9/11 and having Luis were complete luck. But, it is also notable that both Honda and Sushi Zushi had motivation and the capability to take advantage of the luck. Honda had a great technology to build high quality bikes. Alfonso listened to others' advice and took a risk of opening a restaurant just three months after 9/11. He (and his family) worked hard to make their restaurants a fun place to eat sushi.

There are many companies that had luck but were not able to take advantage of it. One example is Goodyear, a tire giant. The years 2000 and 2001 were when one of its main competitors, Firestone, dramatically decreased its sales due to the recall related to the rollover problem with the Ford Explorer. It was a great opportunity to take advantage of the mistakes of a competitor and increase sales and profits. However, Goodyear reported an annual loss for 2001, for the first time in nine years! The loss is mostly attributable to its manufacturing and logistic problems.[16]

Implementing a strategy is dealing with uncertainty and unexpected events. A strategic plan is important, but strategy implementation has different requirements from analysis. Strategy implementation needs learning and improving, as analysis and strategic planning is not an end point, but a starting point. Managers should not be surprised to see their strategy hit a snag. Managers should be ready for unexpected problems and explore opportunities.

In doing so, it is very important to listen to others, customers, rank-and-file employees, and suppliers. They know what is going on in the market. Moreover, information from them should be shared and utilized within an organization through communicating with each other. Additionally, complacency often starts with lack of candid communication.

In sum, strategy implementation cannot be separated from learning and improving. Only continuous efforts to explore opportunities and manage the unexpected lead a company to sustainable success.

EPILOGUE: FROM STRATEGY TO STRATEGIC THINKING

"What three things did you learn from this class?"

I ask this question every time in my last class. Some students immediately respond with such answers as five force framework and 3Cs. Good. My favorite ones include the following:

Trade-off.

Focus.

Uniqueness.

Strategy is strengths. Exploiting strengths rather than fixing weakness.

"Good" or "efficient" is not enough.

Strategic management – managing dilemmas/striking a fine balance of:

- external vs. internal
- finding an opportunity vs. utilizing unique resources
- meeting customers' needs vs. making money
- first-mover advantage vs. first-mover disadvantage
- vertical integration vs. outsourcing
- benefits of acquisition vs. risks of acquisition.

Know (explore) yourself.

Good strategy × good implementation = good outcomes.

Professor Henry Mintzberg emphasizes that strategic programming is different from strategic thinking.[1] He points out that the former is about analysis and decomposition and that the latter is about integration and synthesis. He further argues that for integration and synthesis, intuitions of managers play a very important role. This idea is similar to what Jack Welch calls "a big aha." This text discussed mostly about analyses: how to analyze internal and external environments (3Cs), how to analyze and compare strategic options such as M&As and alliances, etc. It is also pointed out that analyses and subsequent decision making should be as systematic and objective as possible.

Meanwhile, if strategy is all about objective analyses, maybe computers can do most if not all of it. If so, what is the role of managers? Why do so many managers make good money? Most of all, why are there companies that are successful and those that are not successful?

As discussed, analyses are definitely important. Analyses are a foundation of strategy. Unless you make a good analysis, it is highly unlikely that you can come up with a good strategy. However, analyses do not automatically lead to a good strategy and good performance, either. Analysis is a starting point, not a goal. By integrating and synthesizing the results of analyses, managers have to develop a strategy. In this sense, strategy (and management in general) has both science components and art components.

Then, where does the "art" part come from? How can we develop good "intuitions" that play an important role in integrating and synthesizing analyses? In fact, some famous managers including Jack Welch stress the importance of gut feeling.[2]

The answer is not easy. Probably, the following short story can give you some clue.

Mike and Tom met after a 20-year interval. Both of them grew up in the countryside and always played together. Mike stayed in the countryside and Tom graduated from a college and lived in a big town.

When Mike met Tom in his house, Mike heard a bird singing. "Nice," Mike said. "What?" Tom replied. "I did not hear anything." They enjoyed their encounter.

Later, Mike visited Tom and had a dinner with him in a nice restaurant in town. "Didn't you hear anything?" Tom asked. "No," Mike replied. Tom bent over and started searching for something. "Yes!" Tom said. "I found a quarter!"

Intuition and gut feeling will not be explained with a matter of talent. In many cases, intuition and gut feeling are developed through careful thinking and experience. It is reported that talent cannot explain many "geniuses" including musicians, artists, and professional sports players.[3] Instead, it is the many long rigorous practices (e.g., 10,000 hours) that made them "genius." To the extent that our life can be characterized by "believing is seeing," what issues you are interested in and how long and how intense you continue to think the issues determine what intuition you may have.

To this end, strategic thinking will be developed through a sound understanding of basic concepts of strategy and continuous efforts to apply such concepts to the real problems. Joseph Fouché, a French politician who played various roles at the time of the French revolution and has attracted heavy doses of both praise and censure, once said, it is not talent, but a little carefulness and a courage to take actions to be successful as a politician. Probably this idea is also applicable to managers of organizations. A following quote from another French man is appropriate as a concluding remark of this book for future strategists.

Chance favors the prepared mind.
(Louis Pasteur, French chemist and microbiologist, 1822–1895)

NOTES

1 WHAT IS STRATEGY?

1 Hambrick, D.C., and Fredrickson, J.W. 2001. "Are you sure you have a strategy?" *Academy of Management Executive*, 15 (4), 48–59.
2 Mintzberg, H., and Lammpel, J. 1999. "Reflecting on the strategy process" *Sloan Management Review*, spring, 21–30.
3 For more discussion, see Johnson, M.W., Christensen, C.M., and Kagermann, H. 2008. "Reinventing your business model" *Harvard Business Review*, 86, December, 51–59.
4 Welch, J. 2005. *Winning*. New York: HarperCollins.
5 Doran, G.T. 1981. "There's a SMART way to write management's goals and objectives" *AMA Forum*, November, 35–36.
6 "Dell loses its PC lead" *Business Week*, October 20, 2006.
7 "A meeting of the minds: Interview with Peter Drucker" *CIO*, September 15, 1997, 46–54.

2 EXTERNAL ENVIRONMENT ANALYSIS

1 Adamy, J. 2008. "McDonald's takes on a weakened Starbucks" *Wall Street Journal*, January 7.
2 Porter, E.M. 1980. *Competitive Strategy: Techniques for analyzing industries and competitors*. Free Press: New York. Porter, E.M. 1985. *Competitive Advantage: Creating and sustaining superior performance*. Free Press: New York.
3 Please refer to Porter's *Competitive Strategy* and *Competitive Advantage* if you want more detail.
4 Reichheld, F.F., and Sasser, W.E. Jr. 1990. "Zero defections: Quality comes to service" *Harvard Business Review*, September/October, 301–307.

3 INTERNAL ENVIRONMENT ANALYSIS

1 Swisher, K. 2001. "Yahoo! may be down, but don't count it out" *Wall Street Journal*, March 9.
2 Hardy, Q. 1999. "A software star sees its 'family' culture turn dysfunctional" *Wall Street Journal*, May 5.

3 Bulkeley, W.M. 2002. "As PC industry slumps, IBM hands off manufacturing of desktops" *Wall Street Journal,* January 9. Bulkeley, W.M. 2004. "IBM strives deal with rival Lenovo" *Wall Street Journal,* December 8.
4 As technology develops and such information less valuable, Xerox continues to maintain the service department to provide quick service to customers and develop long-term relationships.
5 Forelle, C. 2004. "J.P. Morgan ends accord with IBM" *Wall Street Journal,* September 16.
6 Machida, K. 2008. *Innovation and Uniqueness.* Tokyo: Bungei-shyungyu.

4 BUSINESS LEVEL STRATEGY

1 Porter, P.E. 1996. "What is strategy?" *Harvard Business Review,* November/December, 61–78.
2 Burritt, C., Wolf, C., and Boyle, M. 2010. "Why Wal-Mart wants a driver's seat?" *Business Week,* May 31 to June 6, 17–18.
3 Boudette, N.E. 2003. "At DaimlerChrysler, a new push to make its units work together" *Wall Street Journal,* March 12.
4 Copeland, M.V. 2010. "Reed Hastings: Leader of the pack" *Fortune,* December 6, 120–130.
5 For example, Zook, C. 2001. "Amazon's core problem" *Wall Street Journal,* April 2.
6 Blackwell, R. 2001. "Why Webvan went bust" *Wall Street Journal,* July 16.

5 CORPORATE LEVEL STRATEGY

1 Griffin, N., and Masters, K. 1997. *Hitt and Run.* New York: Simon & Schuster.
2 Green, H. 1984. *Managing.* Garden City, NY: Doubleday.
3 White, J.B., and Shirouzu, N . 2001. "A stalled revolution by Nasser puts a Ford in the driver's seat" *Wall Street Journal,* October 31.
4 Solomon, D., and Rewick, J. 2000. "Why 'bundling' its consumer services hasn't benefited AT&T?" *Wall Street Journal,* October 24.
5 Costas, M.C. 1997. "To diversify or not diversify" *Harvard Business Review,* November/December.
6 Mangalindan, M., and Rhoads, C. 2005. "eBay to buy Skype for $2.6 billion" *Wall Street Journal,* September 13.
7 Fowler, G.A. 2010. "Corporate News: eBay's earnings soar with sale of Skype" *Wall Street Journal,* January 21.
8 Yet, it is reasonable to expect some cost savings (i.e., synergy) in such areas of overhead and information technology investment.
9 Staw, B.M. 1997. "The escalation of commitment" In Z. Shapira (Ed.), *Organizational Decision Making.* 191–215. New York: Cambridge University Press. Shimizu, K., and Hitt, M.A. 2004. "Strategic

flexibility: Organizational preparedness to reverse ineffective strategic decisions" *Academy of Management Executive*, 18 (4), 44–59.
10 *Nikkei Shinbun*, February 28, 2002.

6 M&As, ALLIANCE, AND INTERNATIONAL STRATEGY

1 *Wall Street Journal*, January 2, 2007.
2 Scheck, J., Worthen, B., and DiColo, J.A. 2009. "Dell to buy Perot in catch-up deal" *Wall Street Journal*, September 22.
3 Das, A., and Worthen, B. 2010. "H-P outguns Dell in takeover duel" *Wall Street Journal*, September 3.
4 Das, A., and Tibken, S. 2010. "Dell pulls out of 3Par war with HP" *Wall Street Journal*, September 2.
5 Haunschild, P.R., and Miner, A.S. 1997. "Modes of interorganizational imitation: The effects of outcome salience and uncertainty" *Administrative Science Quarterly*, 42, 472–500.
6 After the 1980s, US car manufacturers learned the importance of cooperation with suppliers. Also, as the demise of Nissan suggests, long-term relationships may not be beneficial when the relationships become too cozy for the partners.
7 Hamel, G. 1991. "Competition for competence and inter-partner learning within international strategic alliances" *Strategic Management Journal*, 12 Special Issue, 83–103. Hamel, G., Doz, Y.L., and Prahalad, C.K. 1989. "Collaborate with your competitors – and win" *Harvard Business Review*, 67 (1), 133–139.
8 Areddy, J.T. 2009. "Danone pulls out of disputed China Venture" *Wall Street Journal*, October 1.
9 Gulati, R. 1995. "Does familiarity breed trust? The implications of repeated ties for contractual choice in alliances" *Academy of Management Journal*, 38 (1), 85–112.
10 Adamy, J. 2006. "Eying a billion tea drinkers, Starbucks pours it on in China" *Wall Street Journal*, November 11.
11 O'Grady, S., and Lane, H. 1996. "The psychic distance paradox" *Journal of International Business Studies*, 27 (2), 309–333.
12 Personal communication, 1994.

7 LEADERSHIP AND DECISION MAKING

1 Hogan, R., Curphy, G.J., and Hogan, J. 1994. "What we know about leadership: Effectiveness and personality" *American Psychologist*, 49 (6), 493–504.
2 Hammond, J.S., Keeney, R.L., Raiffa, H. 1990. *Smart Choices*. Boston, MA: Harvard Business School Press.
3 Ariely, D. 2008. *Predictably Irrational: The hidden forces that shape our decisions*. New York: HarperCollins.

4 Plous, S. 1993. *The Psychology of Judgment and Decision Making.* New York: McGraw-Hill. Bazerman, M. 1998. *Judgment in Managerial Decision Making.* New York: John Wiley & Sons.

5 Hastorf, A.H., and Cantril, H. 1954. "They saw the game: A case study" *Journal of Abnormal and Social Psychology,* 49 (1), 129–134.

6 Coutu, D.L. 2003. "Sense and reliability: A conversation with celebrated psychologist Karl E. Weick" *Harvard Business Review,* 81 (4), 84–90.

7 Welch, J., and Welch, S. 2006. "When to go with your gut" *Business Week,* September 4, 104.

8 Geneen, H., and Moscow, A. 1984. *Managing.* New York: Doubleday Books.

9 Hunter, I.M.L. 1964. *Memory.* Harmondsworth, UK: Penguin Books.

10 For more, see Pfeffer, J., and Sutton, R.I. 2006. *Hard Facts, Dangerous Half-Truths, & Total Nonsense.* Boston, MA: Harvard Business School Press.

11 Covey, S.R. 1989. *The Seven Habits of Highly Effective People.* New York: Simon & Schuster.

12 See Note 10.

13 Thaler, R.H., and Sunstein, C.R. 2009. *Nudge.* New York: Penguin Books.

14 Plous, S. 1993. *The Psychology of Judgment and Decision Making.* McGraw-Hill: New York.

15 Fischhoff, B., Solvic, P., and Lichtenstein, S. 1977. "Knowing with certainty: The appropriateness of extreme confidence" *Journal of Experimental Psychology: Human Perception and Performance,* 3 (4), 552–564.

16 Ball, J., White, J.B., and Miller, S. 2000. "For two car giants, a megamerger isn't the road to riches" *Wall Street Journal,* October 27.

17 Tetlock, P.E. 2006. *Expert Political Judgment: How good is it? How can we know?* Princeton, NJ: Princeton University Press.

18 Hayward, M.L.A., and Hambrick, D.C. 1997. "Explaining the premiums paid for large acquisitions: Evidence of CEO hubris" *Administrative Science Quarterly,* 42 (1), 103–127.

19 Smith, R. 2007. "O'Neal out as Merrill reels from loss" *Wall Street Journal,* October 29.

20 Gigerenzer. G. 2008. *Gut Feeling.* Harlow, UK: Penguin.

21 Lynn, S., Morone, J.G., and Paulson, A.S. 1996. "Marketing and discontinuous innovation: The probe and learn process" *California Management Review,* 38 (3), 8–37.

22 For a good summary, see Staw, B.M. 1997. "The escalation of commitment" In Z. Shapira (Ed.), *Organizational Decision Making,* 191–215. New York: Cambridge University Press.

23 "Will it fly?" *Wall Street Journal,* March 19, 1998.

24 Gersick, C.J. 1994. "Pacing strategic change: The case of a new venture" *Academy of Management Journal,* 37 (1), 9–45. Ghemawat, P. 1991. *Commitment: The dynamic of strategy.* New York: Free Press.

25 Shimizu, K., and Hitt, M.A. 2004. "Strategic flexibility: Organizational preparedness to reverse ineffective strategic decisions" *Academy of Management Executive*, 18 (4), 44–59.

26 Merrick, A. 2007. "Gap will fashion its future without Pressler" *Wall Street Journal*, January 23.

27 Lee, L. 2007. "Paul Pressler's fall from the Gap" *Business Week*, February 26, 80–84.

8 STRATEGY IMPLEMENTATION

1 Tully, S. 2002. "The Jamie Dimon show" *Fortune*, July 22, 88–96.

2 Tuna, C. 2008. "Executives shift to survival mode" *Wall Street Journal*, November 20.

3 Bossidy, L., and Charan, R. 2002. *Execution: The discipline of getting things done*. New York: Crown Business.

4 Neilson, G.L., Martin, K.L., and Powers, E. 2008. "Strategy execution" *Harvard Business Review*, 86 (6), 61–70.

5 Alexander, L. 1985. "Successfully implementing strategic decisions" *Long Range Planning*, 18 (3), 91–97. Mankins, M.C., and Steele, R. 2005. "Turning great strategy into great performance" *Harvard Business Review*, 83 (7): 61–70.

6 Ibid.

7 Sull, D.N. 2007. "Closing the gap between strategy and execution" *Sloan Management Review*, 48 (4), 30–38.

8 Ouchi, W.G. 1980. "Markets, bureaucracies, and clans" *Administrative Science Quarterly*, 25 (1), 129–141.

9 Mehrabian, A. 1971. *Silent Messages* (1st ed.). Belmont, CA: Wadsworth.

10 Sarbaugh-Thompson, M., and Feldman, M.S. 1998. "Electronic mail and organizational communication: Does saying 'Hi' really matter?" *Organization Science*, 9 (6), 685–698.

11 Stasser, G., and Titus, W. 1987. "Effects of information load and percentage of shared information on the dissemination of unshared information during group discussion" *Journal of Personality and Social Psychology*, 53 (1), 81–93.

12 Welch, J. 2005. *Winning*. New York: HarperCollins.

13 Casey, S. 2007. "Patagonia: Blueprint for green business" *Fortune*, May 29.

14 Crossan, M.M., Lane, H.W., and White, R.E. 1999. "An organizational learning framework: From intuition to institution" *Academy of Management Review*, 24 (3), 522–537.

15 Bower, J. 1970. *Managing the Resource Allocation Process*. Boston, MA: Harvard University. Huy, Q.N. 2001. "In praise of middle managers" *Harvard Business Review*, 79 (9), 72–79.

16 Aeppel, T. 2002. "Goodyear, expecting loss of year, may snub car makers" *Wall Street Journal*, February 2.

EPILOGUE: FROM STRATEGY TO STRATEGIC
THINKING

1 Mintzberg, H. 1994. "The rise and fall of strategic planning" *Harvard Business Review*, 72 (1), 107–114.
2 Ibid.
3 For example, Goodwell, M. 2008. *Outliers: The story of success*. London: Little, Brown and Company.

INDEX

Page numbers in *italics* denote tables, those in **bold** denote figures.